ROAD AND RAIL TRANSPORTATION

HISTORY OF INVENTION

ROAD AND RAIL TRANSPORTATION

Harriet Williams

Facts On File, Inc.

Facts On File, Inc.
132 West 31st Street
New York, NY 10001

Library of Congress Cataloging-in-Publication Data

Williams, Harriet
    Road and Rail Transportation / Harriet Williams.
        p. cm.
    Summary: Examines the history of transportation around the world, from prehistoric times when there were not only no wheels but no shoes, to electric, hyrbid cars, and the Global Positioning System.
    Includes bibliographical references and index.
    ISBN 0-8160-5437-1
    1. Roads—History. 2. Roads—History—Pictorial works. 3. Railroads—History. 4. Railroads—History—Pictorial works. [1. Roads—History. 2. Railroads—History. 3. Transportation—History.] I. Title.

HE341.W55 2004
388—dc22

2003047295

Facts On File books are available at special discounts when purchased in bulk quantities for businesses, associations, institutions, or sales promotions. Please call our Special Sales Department in New York at (212) 967-8800 or (800) 322-8755.

You can find Facts On File on the World Wide Web at http://www.factsonfile.com

For The Brown Reference Group plc:
Project Editor: Tom Jackson
Design: Bradbury and Williams
Picture Research: Becky Cox
Managing Editor: Bridget Giles
Consultant: L. Scott Miller, Professor of Aerospace
    Engineering, Wichita State University, Kansas.

Printed and bound in Singapore

10 9 8 7 6 5 4 3 2 1

CONTENTS

WITHOUT WHEELS

Compared to other animals, people are not built for speed or endurance. But we have the imagination and skill to invent technologies that do the hard work for us—machines to harvest food, to build houses, and to turn the most hostile locations into a community.

ON FOOT

In modern times, we take wheels for granted. Spun at high speed by combustion engines, the wheels of cars and buses eat up the miles and allow people to cover long distances quickly and in comfort. In the developed world, the essentials of life are never more than a car trip away. But the wheel is a relatively new tool. For the majority of human history, people had to make do with that most basic of power sources—the human body.

In prehistoric times, people had to travel large distances on foot. There was water and plants to be gathered and animals to be hunted. Many of the hunted

A Nepalese Sherpa carries a load along a snow-covered ridge in the Himalayas. As in other mountain regions, feet are the most effective mode of transportation.

Slip and Slide

Snow presents a unique challenge to people traveling on foot. Sinking with every step into thick snow cover is exhausting and time consuming. The early peoples of Scandinavia overcame these problems with some innovative footwear—skis. Skis are an excellent way of traveling across snow. The wearer's weight is spread over the whole area of the skis, allowing him or her to glide over the surface without sinking.

The first skis appeared about 4,500 years ago in Norway and Sweden. They were made of wood and were covered in animal hair, which was carefully arranged so the hairs pointed backward. This allowed the snow to slide easily over the fur as the ski moved forward. The hair also acted as a brake—when the ski was pushed back, the hairs dug in to give a good grip. In such a way, early skiers could climb hills without wasting energy and slide quickly downhill.

Basic ski design has not changed for millennia, but lightweight, modern skis (above) made from materials such as fiberglass are much faster than those of wood and skin construction. Skiing is now a huge tourist industry, especially in the Rockies and Alps. With the invention of the chairlift in the 1930s, downhill skiing became popular—allowing skiers to enjoy the thrill of the descent without the difficult climb.

animals migrated as the seasons changed, and before the dawn of farming, people in most parts of the world had no choice but to follow them. Any invention that helped people travel more quickly and easily was invaluable.

Without tough pads or hooves to protect them, human feet are easily damaged. So people have been wearing shoes for some 30,000 years. The earliest shoes were simply animal skins tied to the soles of the feet with strips of leather. In colder places, wearers often pulled the skin up around the ankles for warmth.

Modern fashions for high heels or pointed toes may come and go, but the practical design of these early shoes has survived for millennia. By the dawn of the Iron Age—about 3,500 years ago— shoes had developed into a more comfortable and sturdy type of moccasin. Shoes like this are still worn by many people around the world even today.

The basic design of shoe varied according to the local climate. In the Middle East, open-toed leather sandals were an ideal way to protect feet against injury without making them too hot. In Europe

Camel caravans like this have been carrying goods across the deserts of North Africa and the Middle East for many centuries. Camels have since been introduced to Australia for desert travel.

8

A tame elephant pulls a log at a sawmill in southern India. Elephants were the heavy lifters of the ancient world. These intelligent beasts can pick up 600 lbs (270 kg) with their trunks.

Key inventions

Sled Dog Teams

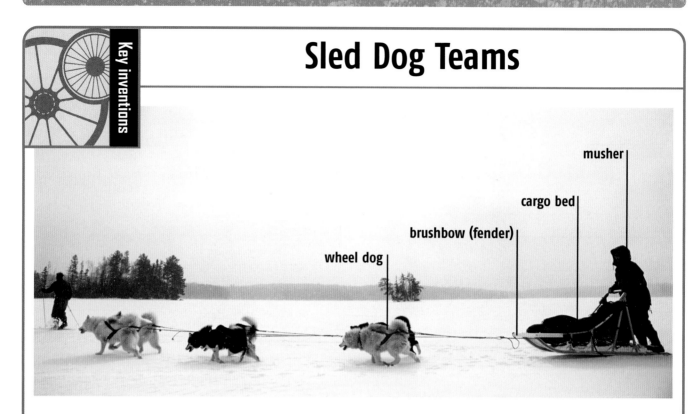

musher

cargo bed

brushbow (fender)

wheel dog

Dogs have been pulling snow sleds for thousands of years. Huskies are the most famous of sled dogs. With exceptionally thick coats to keep out the cold, huskies are more closely related to the wolf than most other breeds of domestic dogs.

The first sleds were made from natural materials such as wood, bone, sinew, and rawhide. Modern sleds are constructed from plastics, steel, and aluminum tubing or carbon fiber. Controlling and steering a dog sled takes skill. With no steering system, the rider, or musher, manages corners by leaning side to side a little like a skier. The fastest mushers also rely on the wheel dogs, which are trained to control the direction for the rest of the team. The sled's brake is a metal claw that the musher digs into the snow.

and Japan, carved wooden clogs were worn to keep the feet dry while working in muddy fields. The availability of materials was a problem in some areas. In China, for example, a country that did not produce much leather, shoes were commonly made of weaker, plant-based fabrics.

With the development of more sophisticated means of travel, the makers of footwear could afford to concentrate on fashion as well as function. Many of today's popular designs, however, have their origins as solutions to real problems. Platform shoes, for instance, were invented in 16th-century Europe to keep ladies' long skirts clear of muddy streets.

In some parts of the world, shoes are still the best way to get around. In the snow-covered regions of Scandinavia, where car tires struggle to find a grip, many short trips are still completed on skis or other modified shoes.

BEASTS OF BURDEN

By 6000 B.C.E., people started to use the power of other animals— that of oxen, donkeys, and other tame beasts—for transportation. People had been hunting animals for food for thousands of years. It is not until 12,000 B.C.E., however, that we find evidence of people harnessing the power of these animals in other ways. At that time, dogs were tamed as hunting partners, but it was another 3,000 years before sheep, goats, and other herd animals were domesticated. They were kept near the base camp as a convenient source of food.

This system of managing food supplies meant that many early peoples did not need to live a nomadic (frequently moving)

Ancient Heavy Lifters

How things work

Powerful vehicles, such as cranes and mobile diggers, make modern construction jobs simple. Precisely how ancient civilizations managed to build their mighty monuments in a time before engines or wheels is still the subject of debate.

The pyramids (above) near Cairo, Egypt, were completed 4,500 years ago. The Great Pyramid (the largest, above right) is made of 2.5 million limestone blocks weighing between 2 and 13 tons (1.8 to 11.7 metric ton) each. The Egyptians and other ancient people probably used a system of rollers to move large blocks many miles from the quarry to the construction sites.

The big question about the pyramids is how the Egyptians hauled the giant stones up to the necessary height. The most popular theory holds that flat-bottomed sleds were used to pull the stones up mud or clay ramps. Some Egyptologists say the ramps were lubricated with water or oil so that sleds could be dragged up easily. Others argue that the sleds were rolled up the ramp aboard long cylinders of wood. In this second scenario, builders would have to continually carry rollers from the back of the sledge to the front. Some theorists claim the Egyptians overcame this problem by fixing a series of rollers along the ramp length. Each roller moved between two roller "stops" as the sled was pulled along.

Any time or energy savings were immensely valuable to the Egyptian workers. The Great Pyramid was completed in just 23 years, giving an average rate of one block being placed every two minutes in a ten-hour working day.

 Fact The Egyptians were not the only ancient people to build pyramids. Native American civilizations from Mexico and Central America built many large pyramids, too.

A Blackfoot family prepare to set off on a journey. They have packed their belongings on a triangular drag, or travois.

lifestyle and could settle in one area permanently. People built the first cities around 6000 B.C.E in Iraq, India, and China. As well as being used for food, large animals were no doubt also used to transport construction material.

Oxen—cattle, yaks, and buffalo—were probably the first animals to be harnessed for transport, followed by tamed asses, or donkeys. In Scandinavia, there is evidence of caribou-drawn sleds from 5000 B.C.E., while camels are the chosen beast of burden in many desert regions to this day. Having evolved to live in arid regions where watering holes are few and far between, camels are perfect for the job, and can carry a heavy load for 30 miles (48 km) a day without water. But the most powerful transporter in

the animal world has to be the elephant. In India, elephants are still used for heavyweight tasks, such as pushing down trees and carrying heavy logs. African elephants, which are larger than their Asian cousins, are too wild to tame and have never been used as beasts of burden.

In these early days of domestication, animals were lashed to a load, and later to wooden sleds, with a simple harness called a yoke. In the case of oxen, these wooden yokes were no more than two pieces of wood shaped as a cross. Two oxen were positioned on either side of the central crossbar. They pushed at the crossbar placed across their shoulders. Oxen and donkeys are still important means of transport in many parts of the world.

Lands Without Wheels

The coming of the wheel heralded a new age for many cultures. This simple invention revolutionized food gathering, building, and warfare in ancient Mesopotamia and Europe but was never developed by the mighty civilizations of the Americas. The Maya, Aztecs, and Incas, who lived from Mexico to Chile, developed some of the most advanced technologies and societies of their time, but why should they fail to develop something so apparently vital as a wheel?

The answer, perhaps, is that the wheel's usefulness is limited in these parts of the world. In places where wheel culture thrived, there was an abundance of strong draft animals to pull wheeled wagons, and it was relatively easy to build decent tracks for them to work on. Amid the steep mountains and dense jungles of Central and South America, the lack of long stretches of flat land limited the potential of wheeled transport. Instead, ancient people in the Americas turned to the solution on their doorstep. Mountain animals such as llamas (a relative of desert camels, above) were the favored mode of transportation. Convoys of these relatively slight animals could move reasonably large loads however steep the terrain.

So wheels are not for everyone, and they are not always used even in parts of the Middle East, where they were first invented. Caravans of camels are still used across the world's desert regions from Morocco to Mongolia. As well as being well suited to crossing endless, dry plains, four-legged camels can also climb up and down fragile sand dunes much more successfully than even the most advanced wheeled vehicles.

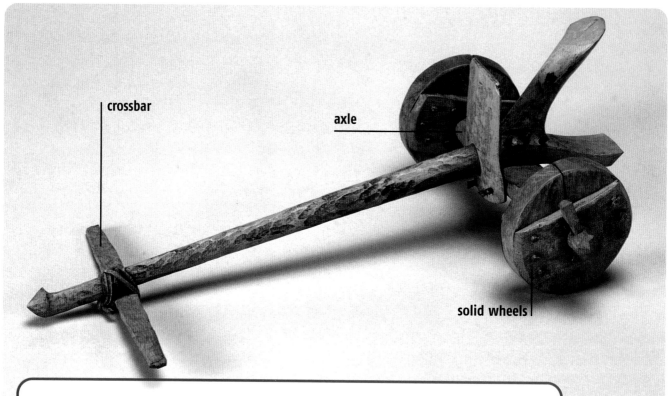

crossbar

axle

solid wheels

INVENTING THE WHEEL

The wheel is among the most significant inventions in human history. Wheels and carts enabled people to travel faster and more comfortably over land, stimulating exploration and trade.

The first wheels are thought to date between 4,000 and 3,500 B.C.E. and come from ancient Mesopotamia (modern-day Iraq) or southern Asia. The concept of moving heavy weights on round objects, such as logs, is older still. The wheel probably evolved slowly from these early rollers.

IN THE GROOVE
Rollers were used in combination with sleds. The load was placed on the sled, which was then pushed over the rollers. People passed an important stage in turning rollers into wheels after realizing that it was easier to move sleds aboard rollers with grooves cut into them. They might have realized this after heavy loads cut into the wooden rollers, making grooves as loaded sleds were rolled over them many times. The circumference (distance around) of the grooved section was smaller than that of the unworn roller. Therefore, dragging the sled across the grooved part took less energy per turn but covered the same distance as the circumference of the roller at its widest point. Cutting away the wood between the grooves created a circular rod—or axle—with wide rollers—or wheels—at each end.

A model of a two-wheeled chariot from about 3,500 years ago. The driver stood above the axle and was pulled along by two horses harnessed to the crossbar.

14

ROLL ON

The first carts were simply boxes or sleds fitted with axles. The axles and wheels at each end were free to turn. Because they were fixed to the cart, the wheels did not roll out from underneath like rollers did.

Wheelwrights—craftsmen that made wheels—did not carve the wheels and axle from a single piece of wood. They joined two semicircles of wood together to make the round wheels, leaving a hole at the center to fix the axle. In a later development, inventors created the fixed axle. In this system the axle does not turn but is fixed to the cart frame for extra strength and stability. The wheels were free to move on the ends of the axle. This is the way almost all wheeled vehicles work today. Solid wooden wheels were eventually replaced with lighter hollow wheels that had spokes connecting a central hub with a solid wheel rim.

This diagram shows the similarity between grooved rollers and an axle with wheels. Wheels are not just used for transportation. They are also used in pulleys, gears, and other simple machines.

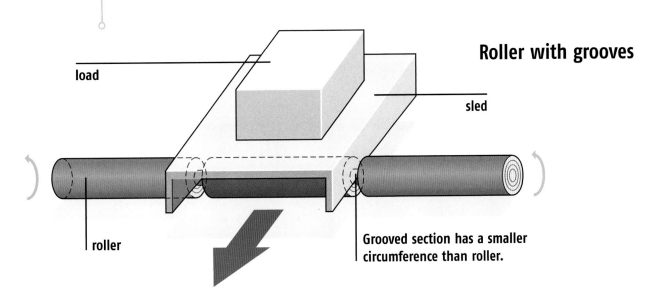

Roller with grooves

load

sled

roller

Grooved section has a smaller circumference than roller.

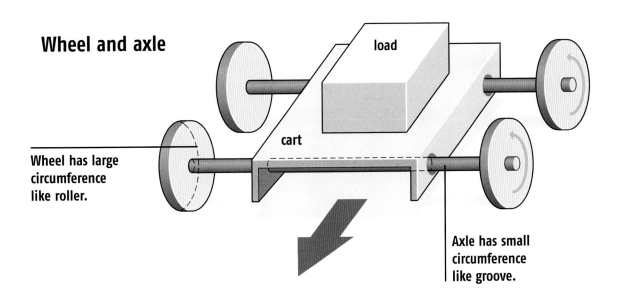

Wheel and axle

load

cart

Wheel has large circumference like roller.

Axle has small circumference like groove.

HORSE POWER

From 3000 B.C.E. to the coming of the railroads in the 19th century, the best way to travel long distances quickly was on horseback. The first horse riders hailed from nomadic societies living on the grassy plains of Central Asia around 5,000 years ago. These grasslands were also home to large herds of horses; strong, graceful animals that could run long distances at speeds of about 30 mph (48 km/h). The nomads rode tamed horses over large areas in search of grazing and, like the cowboys of the American West, rounded up their livestock on horseback.

These early riders did not travel in much comfort. Instead, they rode bareback, gripping on to the horse with their knees and using a strap of leather or knotted grass to steer their mounts. Later on, riders placed animal skins over their horse's back to create a basic saddle, making it easier to cling on to a galloping steed.

WAR HORSES
The Hyksos people, who lived in Palestine 4,000 years ago, had more violent plans for their horses. They were among the first to learn how to purify iron, and used this breakthrough to make many new weapons. They introduced the horse to the battlefield by combining horse power with wheels to create a very effective fighting machine—the chariot.

The Hyksos chariot had two light, spoked wheels made of wood and strengthened with iron. Hyksos charioteers fired arrows into enemy foot soldiers before making a fast getaway. They helped build a Hyksos empire and even managed to defeat the mighty army of ancient Egypt.

The pinnacle of horse-drawn transportation was the mail coach, such as this one from 1830s England. These vehicles could reach speeds of about 10 mph (16 km/h) over long periods. Tired horses were replaced at posts along the road.

By 1300 B.C.E., the Hyksos had invented the bit, a means of controlling horses used by riders to this day. The first books on horsemanship also hail from the Hyksos. They cover breeding, veterinary care, and how to use a chariot properly.

BUILDING EMPIRES

Many other civilizations adopted chariots to use as weapons of war. The Egyptians used them to control the Nile Valley, while the Assyrians, an ancient civilization founded in northern Iraq, used chariots to expand their empire into modern-day Syria, Iran, and Turkey.

The progress of the Assyrian charioteers was blocked by the Zagros Mountains in Iran. Since their two-wheeled vehicles could not climb the uneven tracks, the Assyrians abandoned their wheels and rode across on horseback.

The warriors had to ride into battle, firing their bows at the gallop. However, early domestic

Collar Harness

Key inventions

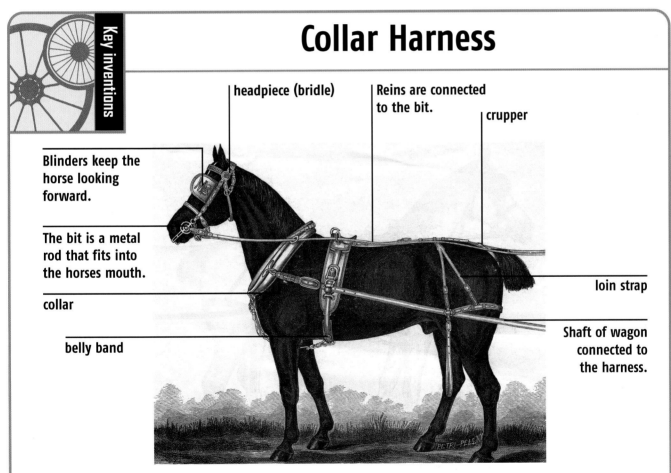

headpiece (bridle)

Reins are connected to the bit.

crupper

Blinders keep the horse looking forward.

The bit is a metal rod that fits into the horses mouth.

collar

belly band

loin strap

Shaft of wagon connected to the harness.

The early days of horse-drawn transportation were uncomfortable for the horse. The first harnesses were simply a bar strapped across the shoulders of two animals and attached to the wagon by a pole. Such harnesses, called yokes, often rode up the horse's neck and pressed on its windpipe.

The collar harness (above) was invented in China, where horses were used to pull wagons, plows, and canal boats. The collar keeps the weight of the load on the horse's shoulders, not on its neck. In this way, a horse in a collar harness can pull up to five times the weight of one in a yoke.

Saddle

Western saddles used in America are similar to the original Sarmatian design.

1. The saddle horn, or pommel, is used as a handle or to tie rope to.

2. The cantle supports the rider's back.

3. The seat is positioned above a pad that protects the horse's back.

4. The fender protects horse's flank, or sides.

5. The rider puts his or her foot in the stirrup.

6. The cinch straps the saddle around the horse.

horses were too small to carry fully equipped soldiers over long distances. So the Assyrians and other ancient peoples began to breed larger animals.

PONY EXPRESS

As the centuries progressed, horses took on more roles. At the height of the Persian Empire between 550 and 330 B.C.E., horses were used for communication as well as war. Royal messengers traveled along newly built roads carrying news to and from every outpost of the empire. A messenger could travel 1,500 miles (2,400 km) in just one week, exchanging tired horses for fresh ones along the way.

Despite the distances traveled by Persian horsemen, it was not until 600 B.C.E. that the first genuine saddle appeared. These were invented by the Scythian people of southern Russia. They were made of padded leather and felt, supported by hoops of wood and belted around the horse's belly. Besides giving a more comfortable ride, the Scythian saddlemakers had fighting in mind. The saddle made a stable seat from which soldiers could accurately aim and fire arrows.

Modern saddles are built around wooden frames, stuffed with padding, and covered with leather. In the first and second centuries C.E., a nomadic Asian people called the Sarmatians had the same idea. They built the first wooden-framed saddles with arches to fit around the horse's back. High peaks at front and rear held the rider in securely, all the better to help the horseman use a heavy weapon, such as a lance. The stirrup was invented at the same time as the Sarmatian saddle. Riders stand on these frames when mounting their horses and can stand up while on the move.

Although the bit, reins, saddle, and stirrup are still the essentials of horsemanship today, modern riders have a range of equipment to choose from for different events. There are different bridles for racing, jumping, and dressage (a very controlled form of riding), and just as many types of saddle. The most complex bridle is saved

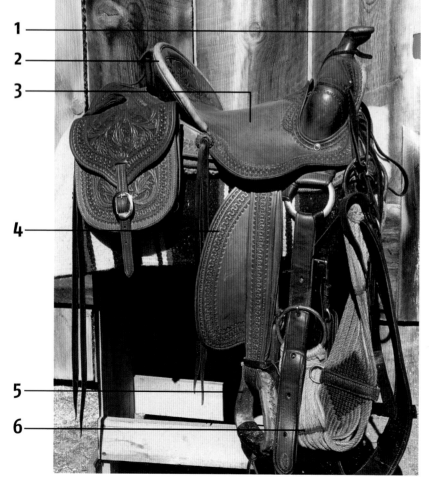

Horseshoes

Riders have to protect their steeds against sore hooves; after all, a healthy horse is a fast one. While horses' hooves are naturally hard enough to deal with off-road riding, hard roads tend to wear them down. In Roman times, people covered their horses' feet with leather and metal sandals. By the sixth century C.E., Europeans had learned to nail metal shoes to hooves without causing pain to the animal. The earliest shoes were cast from bronze, and became widespread by the 11th century. Bronze was eventually replaced with more durable iron shoes.

Horseshoes were so important to people's livelihoods that at many points in history, they were used as money and were even accepted by tax collectors. A whole profession grew up around horseshoes that survives to this day. The word *farrier* was coined in the 16th century to describe the men that nailed shoes to hooves (left).

Invention never stands still, and today's riders can equip their mounts with rubber horse "boots," which protect the legs against sharp objects and mud. Racehorses wear lightweight aluminum shoes to keep their weight down.

for dressage competitions. It involves two bits, each with its own pair of reins. By adjusting both pairs, a rider can send precise directions to his or her horse to change speed and perform complex maneuvers, such as walking sideways.

GO CART!

In contrast to the inventions appearing on top of the horse, the basic design of horse-drawn carts changed little between Roman times and the 16th century. During this time, carts were little more than a wooden box with a wheel at each corner. With no suspension, most people preferred to travel on horseback than bounce along uneven roads.

Surprisingly, an invention that would have radically improved cart design had been forgotten. The Celts of western Europe had used a movable front axle for better steering as early as 50 B.C.E. It was not until the 15th century that wagon builders in the village of Kocs, Hungary, rediscovered this idea. They also made the front wheels smaller, which made the vehicles more stable and easier to turn.

The Hungarians also invented suspension. They hung the body of the cart between the axles rather than resting it on top. This stopped every bump in the road from jolting the passengers. The *kocsi* design, or coach, was common by the 16th century.

WAGONS ROLL!

A large train of wagons takes homesteaders across the prairies in their journey to the west. The pioneers' covered wagons were dubbed "prairie schooners" and were similar to the cart design used by German farmers in Pennsylvania.

Wagons and coaches were the vehicles that brought pioneers to the American frontier. Families in search of a new life in the West carried all their belongings in high-wheeled, covered wagons pulled by up to 20 oxen or mules. (A mule is a strong beast that is a cross between a male donkey and a female horse.) For desert journeys, some travelers used imported camels to pull their loads.

The pioneers followed well-trodden routes, such as the Oregon or Santa Fe Trails, and often covered up to 100 miles (160 km) in a week. For safety, the wagons moved in groups, or trains. A typical wagon train had 25 wagons. Each train was led by a bullwhacker, who guarded the migrants and their belongings. At night, the wagons formed a circle to make a protected area inside in case bandits or warring Native bands attacked.

COACH TRAVEL

Once the frontier had been settled and trading posts and towns established, people traveled by stage coach. Stage coaches were so called because the journey was split into short stages, allowing the horses to be changed or rested. They were the first long-distance passenger services. Coaches were running from London to Edinburgh in Britain in the 1670s, and services were introduced to North America in the 1730s.

Like the wagon trains, there was safety in numbers, as passengers often had to defend themselves when traveling across the American West. A guard sat beside the driver at the front of the coach, generally armed with a shotgun. This is where the phrase "to ride shotgun" comes from.

LONG JOURNEY

One of the most famous stage coach lines was the Butterfield Overland Mail, which ran across prairies, deserts, and mountains from St. Louis, Missouri, to San Francisco, California. This 2000-mile (3,200-km) journey took around 20 days.

The coaches traveled at around 5 mph (8 km/h) and passengers were carried in comfort on springed seats. However, the coaches were on the move day and night, in all weather. Every ten miles (16 km) or so, the coach stopped at a station, where the horses and passengers could eat and drink.

Men in the Wild West prepare to set out on a stage coach. It cost more to travel in relative comfort inside the coach, with less wealthy passengers sitting on the roof with the luggage.

BUILDING ROADS

Roads are an essential part of any developed society. From the great ancient empires to modern-day nation states, countries have always needed ways of moving goods, armies, and people.

Ancient roads are named for the goods that traveled upon them. This includes the Amber Route from Afghanistan to Egypt, and the Silk Route, which stretches 8,000 miles (12,800 km) from China, across Asia and Europe, to Spain. For hundreds of years, generations of tradespeople used slow animals to haul bulky goods along rough, unpaved tracks.

These poor roads vastly increased the price traders charged for goods, since they could not make many trips every year.

ROAD BUILDING
The Assyrians—often called the "Romans of Asia" for their engineering prowess—started the first organized road building in 1115 B.C.E, and continued for 500 years. Their army used roads to travel around quickly, and this helped the empire to grow.

The undisputed champions of ancient road building, however, were the Romans. The Roman

The stone surface of this Roman road, known as the Appian Way, has survived since it was built in 312 B.C.E. The Appian Way was about 350 miles (560 km) long and was the main route between Italy and Greece.

22

travel philosophy was simple—keep it straight. Rather than waste time going around hills, the Romans cut through them, and built bridges, or viaducts, to cross rivers.

Even by today's standards, Roman roads were superbly constructed. They were composed of a graded soil base, topped by a layer of sand, rows of large, flat stones, a thin layer of gravel mixed with lime, and finally a thin surface of hard stone. At the peak of Roman power in the 1st century C.E., the empire maintained some 53,000 miles (84,800 km) of roads from Britain to Egypt. Many Roman roads have been resurfaced several times and are still in use today.

In South America, the Inca people were also skilled road builders. They built causeways through swamps and cut steps up the sides of the steep Andes mountains of Peru and Bolivia.

A NEW DESIGN

By the 18th century, the roads of Europe had fallen into disrepair. Bumpy surfaces frustrated traders and travelers alike. The problem was solved in Britain with the introduction of the turnpike system. Companies were invited to build stretches of road and charge travelers for using them. A long pole, or pike, was laid across the road and turned to allow paying travelers to pass.

Construction workers lay asphalt on a new road. The roller on the right is flattening the hot asphalt into a tightly packed, waterproof surface.

How things work

Modern Road Design

Base: Stone or concrete supports the road surface and stops water seeping up from underneath.

Road markings show drivers where the lanes are.

Shoulders. Used for stopping beside high-speed roads. May be "hard" like the road surface, or "soft" and surfaced with loose gravel.

Subgrade: This is the natural soil that has been packed into a firm base.

Surface: Made from either bitumen or concrete, the surface is smooth and repels water.

Modern road builders often have to clear rock before they start. Explosives are used to blast through hillsides, and the rubble is used to build banks beside the new road. Machines called graders use heavy steel blades to scrape the road smooth, ready for paving. The surface is then pressed down into a solid block by a giant roller.

Modern roads have to serve several functions. Along some roads, people will be stopping cars for schools and stores, while other are purely built for speed. Engineers generally classify three types of road: local, secondary, and primary highways. Local roads typically take vehicles to homes and businesses and generally have many pedestrians on the sidewalk and crossing the road. Therefore they are designed for low, safe speeds, and traffic may be slowed by humps built across the road.

Secondary roads connect local roads to the highways. Highways are built with several lanes in each direction that allow vehicles to travel at

much higher speeds. The surfaces have to be much stronger and are often reinforced with steel rods especially at raised areas (above). Highways are as straight as possible so drivers can maintain high speeds in safety.

✳ Fact The Pan-American Highway is a road that joins Alaska to Chile. The 29,525-mile (47,516-km) road, however, has a short gap in the forests of Panama.

Tunneling Shield

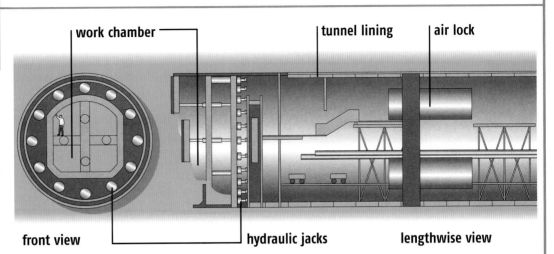

work chamber

tunnel lining

air lock

front view

hydraulic jacks

lengthwise view

This machine was used to dig large road tunnels through soft or wet earth, such as under rivers. It was developed by British engineer Henry Greathead in 1869. The shield was a large, hollow cylinder, in which the tunnelers worked. The air in the shield was under pressure to prevent water from filling it. As the tunnelers dug away the soil in front of the shield, powerful jacks pushed the shield into the now empty space. As the shield moved forward, other workers lined the new tunnel behind it with bricks or concrete slabs. Tunneling shields like this were used until the 1950s, when mechanical tunnel-boring machines replaced them.

Road builders began to search for new, less expensive ways of making smooth and hard surfaces. Their needs were answered by two Scottish engineers—Thomas Telford (1757–1834) and John MacAdam (1756–1836). Telford was the greatest construction engineer of his age. He built many straight and well surfaced roads that ran through cuttings in hills, along raised embankments, and over great river bridges. Telford's system of road building involved digging a trench that was filled with a solid foundation of heavy rocks, covered with 6 inches (15 cm) of gravel. Telford also raised the center of the road into a slight curve, or camber, so that water drained away to the sides easily and did not form puddles on the road's surface.

MacAdam's approach, however, was completely different. He believed in lightweight designs, and did not use stone foundations when the land was well drained enough. Instead his roads had a base of small stones laid onto the ground. This was covered with a layer of finer grained stones. MacAdam improved the gravel surface with the addition of thick tar, or asphalt. This mixture came to be known as tarmacadam, and is still called "tarmac" today.

Although MacAdam's roads were cheaper and faster to build than Telford's design, they were easily damaged by heavier vehicles. Despite this, MacAdam's design persists. A stronger concrete base is generally used instead of stones, but today's roads are still built in much the same way.

Bridge Construction

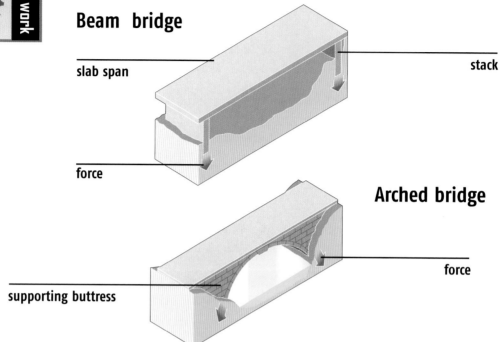

Beam bridge

slab span

stack

force

Arched bridge

supporting buttress

force

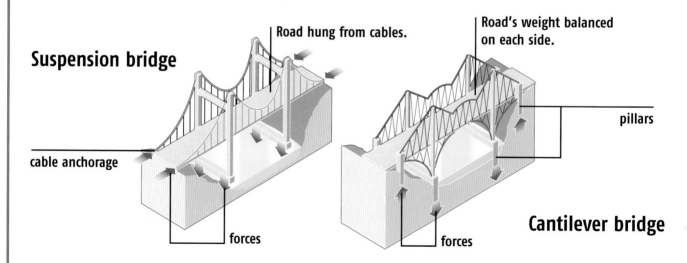

Suspension bridge

Road hung from cables.

cable anchorage

forces

Road's weight balanced on each side.

pillars

forces

Cantilever bridge

People have been building bridges since 2000 B.C.E. The earliest were simple beam bridges—wooden or stone slabs supported on stacks at each end. With the invention of new construction techniques and materials, bridge builders became more ambitious. Arched bridges made from blocks of stone are a hallmark of the Roman era. The inventors of the suspension bridge are unknown. The first of these bridges were likely to have consisted of a wooden deck hung from two ropes slung across the gap.

Modern suspension bridges, such as the Golden Gate Bridge, in San Francisco (right), are held up by super-strong cables. The cantilever bridge was invented in Asia.

All bridge builders face the same challenge: How to transfer the weight of the road and its users into the supports. In wide, modern bridges cables or cantilevers bear most of the weight. Primitive beam bridges are the most vulnerable, and so can only be used across narrow divides.

PEDAL POWER

Bicycles are two-wheeled vehicles that are pedaled by the rider. Bikes like the ones used today became popular at the beginning of the 20th century, around the same time as cars. Being much cheaper than cars or horses, bikes quickly became a popular form of private transportation. Despite many people in wealthy countries replacing their bicycles as soon as cars became more affordable, the humble bike is still the most common vehicle in many parts of the world. As congestion in our cities slows car traffic to a crawl, more people are getting back on their bikes, and bicycle lanes are now a feature of many modern road systems. These lanes are defined by painted lines and distinctively colored asphalt; they allow bicycle and car users to share the same road safely. However, many people are still reluctant to cycle on roads because of the dangers posed by speeding cars. Instead, cycling away from busy roads has become a popular leisure activity.

THE FIRST BIKERS

The earliest cyclists did not have it easy either, having to contend with horse-drawn carriages on uneven roads, and bicycles with no pedals. The first bike to gain popular appeal was developed by German inventor Karl von Drais in 1817. Von Drais attached two wheels together with a pole. By straddling the pole, the rider

Cycling is a very popular sport. Competitors either race each other at high speed on an oval track called a velodrome or race over long distances along roads. The most famous long-distance race is the **Tour de France** *(above) in which superfit cyclists ride all over the country.*

was able to push the contraption along with their feet. This so-called *Laufmaschine,* or "running machine," had basic handlebars and was made of wood.

Laufmaschines quickly became fashionable in Europe and the United States. Enthusiasts had the same trouble learning to balance as many do today, so a series of schools were opened for wealthy cyclists to learn the skill.

Von Drais' bike was improved by English carriage-maker Dennis Johnson. He built lighter and stronger vehicles using metal tubes. Better known as the "hobby horse," Johnson's *pedestrian curricles* quickly knocked the *Laufmaschine* off the streets.

Still, however, there were no pedals. Ironically, the first design for a pedal bike may have already been created in the 15th century by the Italian genius Leonardo da Vinci (1452–1519). Famous for his art, da Vinci was a proficient engineer too. A manuscript from the 1490s appears to show a da Vinci drawing of a two-wheeled cycle with pedals and a chain

drive attached to the back wheel. This idea was subsequently lost and was not replicated until the end of the 19th century. The first pedal bike, invented by Scottish blacksmith Kirkpatrick MacMillan, did not use a chain either. Instead the pedals were connected by cranks (crooked shafts bent at right angles) to the rear wheel.

The pedal bike was improved still further in the 1860s when French carriage maker Pierre Lallement attached pedals and cranks to the front wheel of a hobby horse. With their feet freed from the ground, bike riders were now able to pick up speed. Lallement's machines were called *velocipedes.* They surpassed all previous designs in popularity, and the first *velocipedes* race was held in Paris in 1868.

CHAIN REACTION

The age of cycle racing was born, and inventors began to design faster bicycles. In the days before gears, the only way to make a faster bike was to fit it with larger wheels. Larger wheels covered more ground than smaller ones for each turn of the pedals.

The most famous type of these newer, faster bicycles was the penny farthing. This bike, designed by Englishman James Starley in the 1870s, was really named *The Ordinary* but earned its more familiar nickname because its front wheel was so much larger than the back, resembling the old British penny and farthing coins.

Many people found the penny farthing difficult to use. Short people could not reach the pedals,

An early cyclist takes a ride, pushing himself forward with his feet. This early bicycle was known as the "bone shaker" because it was such an uncomfortable ride.

Racing Giants

handlebars

warning bell

saddle

pedals

For anyone in a hurry, bigger was certainly better in the days of penny farthing bicycles (above). The front wheel turned once for every pump of the legs, and the cycle moved forward the length of one circumference of the wheel. So, it made sense to ensure that the wheel was large enough to cover a substantial amount of ground. The front wheel of racing penny farthings were anything up to 60 inches (152 cm) in diameter. In fact, the only restriction on the size of wheel was the length of the rider's legs. Because of this, the first cycling champions were all very tall. In the 1880s, the 6 foot 2.5 inches (1.8 m) of English racer Herbert Lidell Cortis triumphed in most of the major race meetings. The back wheel of the penny farthing was tiny by comparison, to keep the contraption's weight down. The back wheel's one crucial function was to stabilize the bike.

while women could not ride for fear their skirts would be caught in the long wheel spokes. And for every rider it was a long way to the ground if they fell off.

Starley's nephew, John Kemp Starley, set about designing a safer bike. In 1885, he introduced the *Rover Safety*. The *Safety* had pedals that turned a chain attached to the rear wheel. It also had simple gears that allowed the back wheel to turn more than once for each turn of the pedals.

Early safety bikes had front wheels slightly larger than the rear ones. However, soon bikes had two wheels the same size. The wheels were hard and rigid and transmitted all the bumps in the road up into the rider's saddle. Air-filled tires changed all this. They were first added after John Dunlop (1840–1921) fitted rubber tubes to his son's tricycle in 1888. (Dunlop went on to set up one of the world's largest rubber companies.) Since then the basic design of chain-driven bikes has barely changed to this day.

DESIGN AND FUNCTION

While basic bike design has not changed for over a century, it has been modified to suit different uses and conditions. Tires are one element that vary. The thick tires and deep grip of a mountain or trail bike make sure a large area of the tire touches the ground at all times. This helps the rider stay upright in uneven or slippery conditions. Racing bikes, however, have narrow tires with little grip. They reduce the surface area in contact with the ground. With

Racer

curved handlebars

thin tires

Trail bike

shock absorber

disk brakes

thick tires

Recumbent

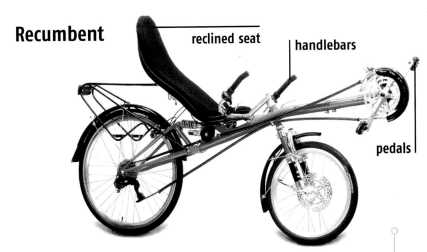

reclined seat

handlebars

pedals

only a tiny amount of tire on the ground, the weight of the rider is focused into a tiny area. This creates very high friction forces between the tire and the ground, which ensures that all the racer's effort is translated into motion.

Several designs of bicycle frame are also available. Trail bikes have strong frames fitted with shock absorbers for a more comfortable

Modern bikes vary greatly depending on what they are used for. Their frames contain light metals, such as magnesium, and tough carbon fibers.

off-road ride. These cycles are fitted with disk brakes, which work by gripping the spinning wheel at its center. Disk brakes give the rider extra stopping power that is not needed on the road. Racing bikes use calliper brakes, which grip the wheel rim.

The frames of modern racing bikes are made from lightweight metal alloys or carbon fiber. Their high saddles and low, curved handlebars allow the rider to crouch down to take a more aerodynamic riding position.

One of the more innovative designs of modern bike is the recumbent cycle. Here, the rider looks as if he or she is lying down. The back rests diagonally against a support over the back seat, while the legs push pedals suspended over the front wheel. The pedals are linked to the back wheel by a long chain. Riders can make long journeys comfortably in this reclining posture. Recumbent bikes are very aerodynamic. They take little effort to ride and are banned from most competitions.

Key inventions

Superbikes

Professional cyclists devote years of their lives to improving their fitness, but they will not break any speed records or win races without the right bike. Whenever an object travels through a fluid (a gas or liquid, such as air or water) it produces drag—a resistance force that slows the object.

Bicycles and their riders are no exception, and competitive racing teams have spent a lot of brainpower on the struggle to reduce drag and move faster than their rivals. When British cyclist Chris Boardman won at the 1992 Olympic Games

in Barcelona, Spain, aboard a low-drag "superbike" (left), the world's cycle designers took notice. Boardman had trained inside a wind tunnel to monitor how air flowed over his body and to make sure he adopted the most aerodynamic riding position. He also wore an elongated crash helmet to reduce drag, and the spokes of his bike's rear wheel were covered to cut down on resistance as it sliced through the air.

Soon all the top riders were using superbikes, but each new innovation made competitive cycling more about bike design than tactics and human muscle power. The sport's governing body made many superbike features illegal to maintain fair competition, and any new alterations to racing bikes are reviewed carefully.

Derailleur Gears

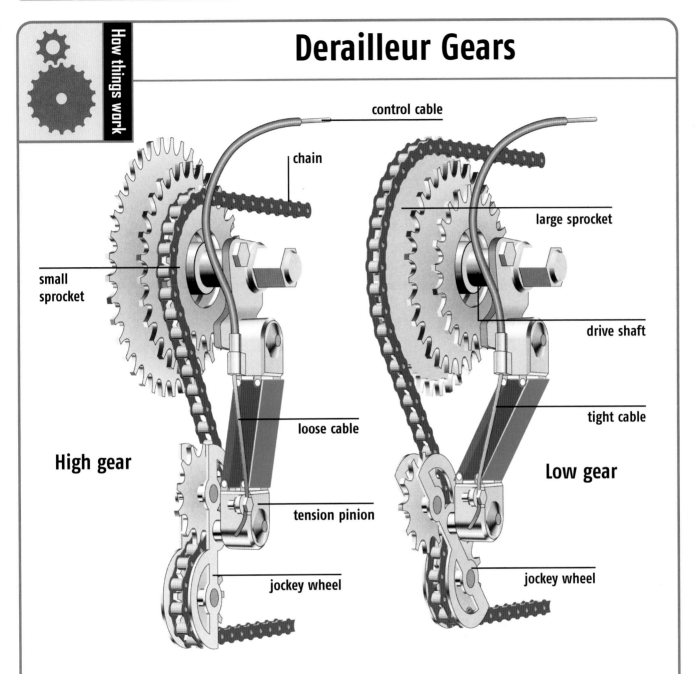

control cable

chain

small
sprocket

High gear

loose cable

tension pinion

jockey wheel

large sprocket

drive shaft

tight cable

Low gear

jockey wheel

Gears make a cyclist's life much easier, helping him or her climb up steep hills or reach high speeds. The modern type of derailleur bicycle gear was invented in 1911. These gears consist of a series of different-sized cogs, or sprockets, which are attached to the drive shaft of the rear wheel. The chain attaching the cogs to the pedals grips the teeth of a cog, turning it as the cyclist's legs turn.

The amount that the bike wheels spin with every turn of the pedals depends on the size of the gear cog in use. If the chain is turning a large cog, the bike only moves a small distance with every turn of the pedals but with more power, so

pedaling is easier. Low gears like this help riders cycle uphill with a minimum of effort. High gears are more appropriate for flat areas, where the rider is not fighting against gravity. In high gear the chain turns a small cog. With every turn of the pedals, the bike's rear wheel rotates several times, helping the rider travel faster.

Cyclists using derailleur gears adjust a lever near the handlebars to change gear. The lever tightens or loosens a control cable connected to two smaller wheels next to the gear, called jockey wheels. These wheels move in and out, guiding the chain on and off the different-sized gear cogs.

THE FIRST TRAINS

From its humble beginnings in 16th century Europe, rail travel gradually spread across the world. At the peak of the rail era, there were more than a million miles (1.6 million km) of track. A quarter of all these tracks were in the United States alone. Since then, rail transportation has been largely replaced by road vehicles, but trains are still an inexpensive and fast way of moving cargo and passengers over long distances.

MAKING TRACKS

The first rail tracks, however, were not put down with passenger trains in mind. They were laid around the mines that produced coal or iron ore in 16th-century Europe. In 1550, when these first rails appeared, no inventor had yet conceived the idea of an engine, let alone the concept of a whole train. Horses were used to pull carts along the rails instead.

Hauling heavy wagons over rough ground is hard work and time consuming. Rolling them along a pair of raised and smooth rails, however, is much easier. The first rails were made of wood and covered only short distances from the mouth of the mine to a loading point. The weight of laden wagons quickly wore the wood down. Engineers started nailing strips of iron to the rails to make

Richard Trevithick's **Catch-Me-Who-Can** *steam engine runs around a circular track in London in the summer of 1808. Trevithick brought his 8-ton (7.2-metric ton) engine to the city as a tourist attraction in the hope that he would get support for his railroad plans.*

34

them more hard-wearing, before eventually switching to rails made of solid iron. The first metal rails were laid in England in 1738, but this did not solve all problems.

How to get a wagon from one track to another without enormous manual effort was a headache for mine operators. A solution came in 1789 when English engineer Williams Jessop invented a switch, or points, system. Points, which are still used on modern railroads, are short lengths of rail that taper to a point at the end. These pointed rails switch a train from one track to another running alongside it. They are operated by signalmen, and initially, these operators moved the points between tracks by hand. More modern points systems are powered by electric motors, or hydraulic systems that use compressed air.

Tracks outside a railroad station are linked by points. The pointed rails make it possible to connect parallel tracks to one another.

ENGINE START UP

With sturdy iron rails and a means of changing track, the stage was set for the invention of the first trains. The first steam-powered vehicles to run on rails were built by Richard Trevithick (1771–1833), an English engineer. Trevithick's train used the steam from boiling water to move pistons and turn the wheels. Others suggested that the engine would move best if it was fitted with coglike, toothed wheels, running on toothed rails. However, Trevithick defied his critics and fitted his first rail locomotive with smooth wheels, which managed to grip smooth rails tightly. (Smooth rails are easier to produce.)

While earlier designs of steam engine had failed to produce enough power to turn wheels under the huge weight of the engine, Trevithick's boiler was efficient enough to produce steam at the high pressure needed to generate sufficient force. In 1804, one of Trevithick's locomotives pulled five wagons loaded with 11 tons (10 tonnes) of iron over 9.75 miles (14 km) of track. Dozens of spectators came along for the ride. With an average speed of about 5 mph (8 km/h), Trevithick's train seems very slow, but at the time, it was a sensation.

CRACKING RAILS

A range of technological problems still had to be overcome before railroads could be an efficient and widespread form of transportation. For example, iron rails frequently shattered under the huge weight of a steam engine. Nonetheless, Trevithick continued to promote his vision for rail transportation. In 1808, he constructed a railroad engine to demonstrate the potential of steam power. Called the *Catch-Me-Who-Can*, this engine pulled a small train around a circular track carrying passengers at a shilling (about 10 cents) a ride. But ticket sales were not brisk, and Trevithick soon went bankrupt. He spent his later years in South America, installing his powerful steam engines in silver and gold mines there.

Iron rails were replaced with tracks made out of tougher steel, and the first practical railroad opened between the English towns of Leeds and Middleton in 1812. The locomotives hauled coal along toothed rails rather than smooth ones at very slow speeds.

FOUNDING FATHER
Perhaps the most famous railroad pioneer is the English inventor George Stephenson (1781–1848).

People and society

Horse-Drawn Rail Cars

In the earliest days of rail, horses were used to haul the wagons (above). Many of the first passenger railroads were also horse-drawn. Horse-powered trains even outlasted the introduction of steam engines at the start of the 19th century. With relatively few locomotives in service, railroad owners bought up many thousands of horses to move rolling stock around rail yards, unload cars, and take freight on to its destination. As late as 1928, Britain's London Midland and Scottish Railway still owned nearly 10,000 horses. The very last horse-drawn passenger service, in Fintona, Northern Ireland, operated until 1957.

Puffing Billy

Puffing Billy (above) was the locomotive that showed the world that trains could haul heavy loads. Its inventor was William Hedley (1773–1843), who was working to improve the transportation of coal—the fuel that powered the Industrial Revolution. In 1808, Hedley worked out how to couple smooth rails and smooth wheels firmly using a flange (rim) on the wheel. *Puffing Billy* was completed in 1813 and hauled coal wagons in England. After the track was damaged by the train's weight, the original rails were strengthened with cast iron edges. This was enough to keep *Puffing Billy* in service until 1862, when the train was retired to a museum in London.

A former firefighter, Stephenson constructed his first locomotive, *My Lord*, in 1814, which ran at just 6 mph (9.6 km/h)

As railroads were built across more of Britain, Stephenson's advice was frequently sought. He was just as particular about standards in railroad construction as he was about the locomotives themselves. He insisted on tracks being laid in well-prepared beds to allow more trains to travel at higher speeds. Where the track turned, for example, the engineer insisted on a curve of no less than half a mile (0.8 km) in radius to help the train travel safely around the bend. Stephenson's techniques were sound, and most railroads in other countries were built to a similar design.

FATHER OF RAIL

Until the 1820s, railroads were built and controlled by mining companies. After improving the design of steam engines, however, George Stephenson was made chief engineer of the first true passenger railroad, the Stockton to Darlington Railway in northeast England. When completed in 1825, this new line was open to anyone for carrying cargo and passengers.

The success of the Stockton to Darlington link led to a much bigger project—a railroad linking the cities of Manchester and Liverpool. After several problems during construction, the new railroad

George Stephenson at the controls of Locomotion, *the engine he built for the Stockton and Darlington Railway, during the first journey along the railroad in 1825. The engine pulled 36 wagons and was followed by hundreds of spectators.*

opened in 1830. Stephenson had not lost his interest in engine design, and he won a competition to build the most suitable locomotive for the new railroad.

Stephenson's engine, which was mainly designed by his son Robert (1803–59), was christened *Rocket*. *Rocket* used a powerful design of boiler which gave the engine a top speed of 36 mph (58 km/h)— a huge leap forward at the time. The engine's speed was thanks to its "steam-blast" boiler. This directed jets of steam through a blast pipe into the locomotive's chimney, causing air to be sucked in after it. The air draft created fanned the flames in the boiler's furnace, making it hotter. The hotter furnace produced steam at a very high pressure, capable of driving an engine faster than ever.

Stephenson went on to build the world's first railroad network in central England, and his legacy remains: The gauge (distance between rails) he adopted has become the standard around the world.

As well as building engines and tracks, George Stephenson was also a skilled construction engineer. Here, he is pictured with plans for a viaduct (bridge) he was building to carry a raiload.

THE AGE OF STEAM

The first long distance railroads were built in Britain in the 1820s. The railroads changed the lives of ordinary people, most of whom had never had the opportunity to travel more than a few miles from home. By the 1840s, trains were carrying up to 2,400 passengers at a time to faraway places.

Train operators urgently needed new ways to manage the traffic on the railroads. In 1841, semaphore signals were introduced in London so that signalmen communicated with drivers using flags. Signalmen also used electric telegraph machines to send messages down trackside wires to keep each other up to date on train movements.

There was obvious value in making tracks of one standard width, or gauge, and here, the legacy of George Stephenson lived on. He laid rails 4 feet 8.5 inches (1.44m) apart. This width became a global standard, and today two-thirds of tracks follow this gauge. One famous exception was Britain's Great Western Railway built by engineer Isambard Kingdom Brunel (1806–59), who believed that wider tracks would be more stable at high speed.

U.S. RAILROADS

By 1850, Britain had 4,000 miles (6,500 km) of railroad, with 2,500 steam locomotives. Compared to the slow pace of previous transportation systems based on horse power, Britain's railroad seemed to have it all. But across the Atlantic Ocean, American inventors had begun to

A rail gang lay track as part of the construction of the Union Pacific Railroad. Railroads bought people and new technologies to parts of North America that had been only seldom visited before by non-Native settlers.

outpace European developments. The first steam-powered passenger line in the United States opened on Christmas Day, 1830, joining Charleston and Hamburg, South Carolina. It consisted of a 6 mile (9.6 km) stretch of track and a U.S.-designed locomotive named the *Best Friend of Charleston*. The rigorous demands of the North American landscape meant that innovations had to come quickly. Long distances, high mountain ranges, and extremes of climate put engineers under pressure to build more reliable railroads.

The British design of locomotive simply was not up to the job of pulling trains up steep hills and around sharp curves. The design of steam locomotives used in North America had to be more powerful to be reliable and safe. In 1832, American engineer John B. Jarvis built the first train with wheels on swiveling bogies that guided the train into tighter corners. The ability of the train body and wheels to swivel in slightly different directions allowed locomotives to take curves more safely. Jarvis' design was improved in 1865, when the first fully articulated, or jointed, locomotive started to negotiate sharp bends that would have made other cars leave the track.

The American railroads also led the way in passenger comfort. The first sleeping cars ran on the Cumberland Valley Railway in Pennsylvania and Virginia in 1836. Passenger cars with a central aisle were invented for the Baltimore and Ohio Railroad in 1853, and the first dining car was attached to a steam locomotive in 1863.

Poorer people did not travel in such style. The first railroad to cross the United States from the Atlantic and Pacific was completed in 1869, and enormous numbers of migrants headed west to seek

People and society

Traveling in Style

In the early days of rail travel, comfort was simply measured by how far away passengers were seated from the rail car's unsuspended wheels—if they were lucky enough to have a seat, of course. Early rail cars were more often than not empty boxes more suited to the transport of industrial freight or farm animals. This all changed in the 1860s, when U.S. businessman George Pullman (1831–97) moved comfort to the top of a rail traveler's requirements. His first-class sleeping cars were introduced in 1864, followed by dining cars (above) in 1868. Pullman's cars were famed for their comfort across the world, and soon the name *Pullman* was given to any luxury rail car. Pullman exported his design to Europe where wealthy passengers were waited upon as they relaxed in his large upholstered chairs. Perhaps the most luxurious train was the *Orient Express*, which began traveling between Paris, France, and Istanbul, Turkey, in 1882.

their fortunes. Many newcomers' first sight of their new homes was through the windows of overcrowded train compartments, complete with screaming babies, furniture, and livestock.

The U.S. economy received a huge boost through the country's railroad infrastructure. Thousands of people from around the world came to America to labor on the railroads. Towns and cities grew up around railroad stations, as business people began to import and export products by rail.

HIGHER SPEED

In 1876, an express train on the Pennsylvania Railroad set a world record for a steam locomotive by travelling 438 miles (701 km) non-stop from Jersey City, New Jersey, to Pittsburgh, Pennsylvania. In 1893, American rail passengers became the first people to travel at 100 mph (160 km/h), pulled by a New York locomotive named *999*.

High-speed travel was made easier by the invention of the automatic lubricator by African American engineer Elijah McCoy (1843–1929) in the 1870s. Before this innovation, the moving parts of a steam engine

or another type of locomotive had to be lubricated by hand between journeys. McCoy's device lubricated engines as they were working, and allowed train drivers to push their engines harder, attaining higher speeds. Drivers insisted on "the real McCoy" when having a lubricator installed, and people use the same phrase today to mean "the real thing."

LATER YEARS

With higher speeds the need for safe railroads became ever greater. The first block signaling system was invented by the New York and Erie Company in 1849. Signalmen were instructed to allow only

A "Big Boy" locomotive from the 1940s. Its huge engine drove 16 wheels and could reach speeds of 80 mph (129 km/h).

Two engines build up steam on a railroad in India. The sooty smoke produced by engines often makes the passengers seated behind dirty.

successful electric alternative to steam was not developed until the 1880s. By end of the 1940s, most U.S. steam locomotives had been retired from service after many years of service. However, huge steam engines—nicknamed "Big Boys"—were built during World War II (1939–45). The Big Boys were used to pull massive loads of weapons and equipment through mountainous country. These steam locomotives were the largest and most powerful ever built and were used until the 1960s.

one train into each rail length, or "block" at a time. Other advances were made in Europe. In 1856, the first electric signaling systems was introduced on the Paris to Dijon line in France.

By the late 19th century, the steam age was beginning to wane. Train operators were starting to add new, diesel-powered trains to their stock of steam locomotives. In 1839, an experimental battery-powered locomotive was developed in the United States. But the first

But steam power still lives on elsewhere. Vintage locomotives run on scenic lines and are popular tourist attractions. Steam engines are in regular use in parts of Asia and Africa. China only stopped constructing new steam engines at the end of the 1980s.

Key inventions

High-Speed Steam

While the basic technology of steam trains was unchanging, design improvements after 1900 helped locomotives pick up speed. Trains became more streamlined so they cut through the air more easily. Most famous of these sleek locomotives is the *Mallard* (above). In 1938, this British engine reached a speed of 126 mph (202 km/h), while pulling four carriages between Grantham and Peterborough, England. This is the fastest a steam train has ever traveled.

STEAM LOCOMOTIVES

Steam trains are powered by water. When liquid water is heated it becomes water vapor, or steam. To produce steam, locomotives heat a large tank of cold water by burning wood, coal, or oil in a furnace, or firebox.

In turning from liquid to gas, the space, or volume, that the water occupies increases by about 1,600 times. But the steam is not allowed to expand. Instead it is forced into a small volume under high pressure.

The high pressure steam is directed into cylinders on either side of the locomotive.

The hot gas forces pistons inside the cylinders back and forth. The pistons are connected to the locomotive's drive wheels by rods that convert the back and forth

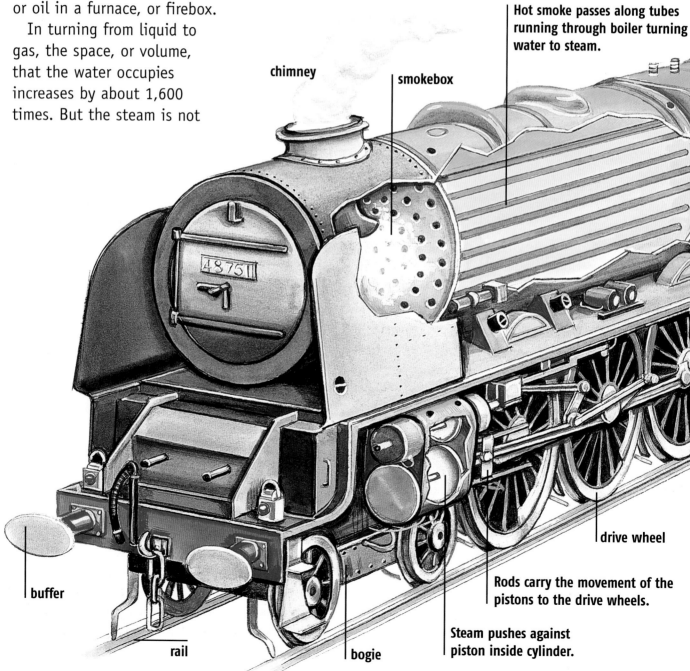

Hot smoke passes along tubes running through boiler turning water to steam.

chimney

smokebox

drive wheel

Rods carry the movement of the pistons to the drive wheels.

Steam pushes against piston inside cylinder.

buffer

rail

bogie

motion into circular motion. Most locomotives have at least six drive wheels, which are larger than the others.

The steam engine owes much of its success to James Watt (1736–1819), a Scottish inventor who patented a steam engine in 1769. Watt overcame previous power problems by installing a steam condenser. This cooled the used steam in a condenser separately from the cylinders. Watt's design saved fuel and was the first to harness the steam to move the pistons in both directions.

Watt compared the power of his engines to the number of horses it would take to do the same job. A 15-horsepower engine, for instance, had the power of 15 horses. (The modern unit of power is not based on horses, but is called a Watt for the inventor.)

Despite being expensive, Watt's innovations paved the way for the steam engine to power the Industrial Revolution in factories, on rail, road, and at sea.

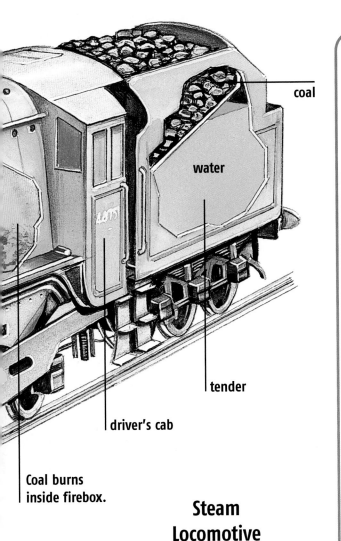

coal

water

tender

driver's cab

Coal burns inside firebox.

Steam Locomotive

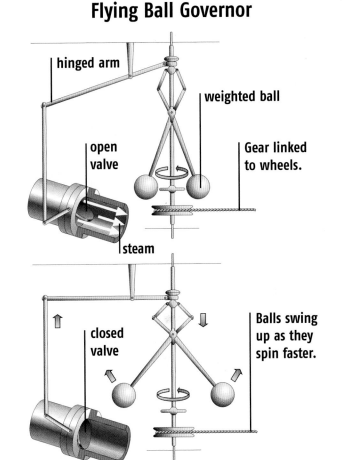

Flying Ball Governor

hinged arm

weighted ball

open valve

Gear linked to wheels.

steam

closed valve

Balls swing up as they spin faster.

Watt used a device called a governor to control his engines. It consisted of two heavy fly balls that spun around as the wheels moved. The balls were linked to a valve that controlled the amount of steam reaching the engine's cylinders. As the wheels turned faster, the balls rose up and closed off the steam valve. With less steam in the cylinders, the wheels began to slow.

MODERN RAILROADS

An intercity train zooms into Chicago. This train has two decks for passenger seats. Most trains on U.S. railroads carry freight rather than passengers.

After the first steam train appeared at the turn of the 19th century, innovations came thick and fast. As the steam era reached its peak, inventors were already looking around for more efficient ways to power locomotives.

INTERNAL COMBUSTION

In 1892, German engineer Rudolf Diesel (1858–1913) designed a powerful type of internal-combustion engine. His engine drove pistons up and down by exploding a type of gasoline in a controlled way. The gasoline fuel is called diesel today.

Diesel engines had obvious advantages over those powered by steam. They do not require much water and turn heat energy from burning fuel into rotational motion more efficiently. The first diesel locomotive ran on a German railroad in 1912. It proved a great disappointment. Although diesel fuel is a good source of energy, the engine was not up to the job of pulling a heavy train.

In the same year, Swedish inventors came up with the idea of coupling a diesel engine to electric power. In diesel-electric locomotives, the diesel engine does not drive the wheels directly. Instead, it drives an electric generator that powers the wheels with electricity. This was the system that eventually replaced steam as the main type of engine power used in North America. Diesel-electric trains were cheap to build, and they could reach high speeds, while using less fuel. Compared to grimy, soot-coated steam engines, they were easier to maintain, too.

MOTOR RAILS
Diesel-powered locomotives were introduced to U.S. and European passenger lines in the 1930s, and were hauling most freight trains

Cable Car

Cable streetcars were invented by Andrew Smith Hallidie (1836–1900), who designed a streetcar system for San Francisco (above) in 1867. Hallidie's cars are attached to a moving cable that ran in a slot between the streetcar's rails. Each car is fitted with grippers to clutch the cable. When he or she wants to stop, the driver detaches the car from the cable and applies a brake. At the time cable cars were a good way of getting passengers up steep hills. By 1900, San Francisco had 100 miles (177 km) of cable car line, and another system served Seattle. But cable cars had many flaws. Cars could only travel at a slow, fixed speed, and a single break in the cable shut down the whole system. Today, the only cable cars still running are a tourist attraction in San Francisco.

by the 1950s. Diesel-electric locomotives, traveling up to 147 mph (237 km/h), pull most of the long-distance trains in Europe and the United States today. Engines pulling heavy loads often need additional diesel-powered booster units behind the main engines to help them travel up hills. On the way down the other side, heavy trains would run out of control without braking cars, often at the rear of the train.

Attempts to improve the diesel–electric formula have not been entirely successful. Gas turbine engines were developed in the 1940s. These used a stream of hot gases to spin a turbine, which generated electricity. However, they were found to be less fuel efficient than the diesel version and these trains have now been taken out of service.

ELECTRIC TRAINS
The first electric-only passenger trains appeared nearly 20 years before the diesel engine was invented. A light railroad powered by electricity opened in Germany in 1881, and by 1902 there were electric locomotives running on lines in Italy. In terms of speed and efficiency, electric trains are even better even diesel-electrics.

Despite their efficiency, electric railroads are very expensive to set up. While steam and diesel locomotives are self-contained power sources, electric trains need to be plugged into a current of electricity for their entire journey. This power is supplied through an electrified third rail or overhead electric cables. The engine picks

Streetcar

Streetcars, or trams, are railroads that run along city roads. The first electric streetcar line was built between Manhattan and Harlem in 1832. Today, most U.S. streetcars have been replaced by bus systems, but they are still a common form of mass transit in Europe.

1. Overhead cables carry the electricity used to power the streetcar.

2. The electric current is collected by the streetcar's pantograph, which connects to the motor.

3. Like a train, the streetcar is controlled by a driver, who follows signals. Passengers get on and off the streetcar at specific stops.

4. Streetcars share the road with cars and other vehicles. Generally, however, streetcars follow their own lanes.

5. The rails are embedded in the road surface so they do not form obstacles for other road vehicles.

up electricity from the third rail through a flattened "shoe" that slides over the surface. Overhead cables are connected by an armlike extension, or pantograph. Both these variations are very expensive to build, but because electric trains produce far less pollution than diesel engines, they are widely used for urban routes near to people's homes.

The most modern electric trains are operated by computer rather than a human driver. Sensors on the track tell the train where it is so it knows to stop at stations. The sensors also tell the computer the positions of the other trains on the track. Automatic trains are often used to move people around airport terminals. Computers are still essential for many trains that have drivers, providing information about the track ahead.

STRAIGHT LINES

The development of rail services owes as much to railroad and track construction as it does to train design itself. The fastest routes have few sharp bends, that would force drivers to slow down. Instead of going around obstacles, engineers building high-speed lines go through or over them. Modern construction techniques allow railroads to span deep ravines or tunnel through mountains. Shallow tunnels are generally deep trenches that are lined with concrete and topped with a concrete roof. But cut-and-cover tunnels, as these are called, are no good for tunneling through mountains or deep underground. Here, giant boring machines are used to drill tunnels with a turning circle of teeth. Progress can be painfully slow. The 31-mile

(50-km) Channel Tunnel between England and France, for instance, was only completed at a rate of 1 mile (1.6 km) a month.

Trains have had to compete with other forms of transportation. Locomotives that reach speeds of over 100 mph (160 km/h) are now common in the developed world. Although road speed limits are much lower, train companies face competition from trucks in the high-stakes world of freight transportation. Roads are less expensive to construct than railroads, and serve a far larger number of destinations. This has led many companies to transport goods by road. Train operators have responded with "piggyback" services—a system that combines the speed and efficiency of rail with the flexibility of road travel by loading trucks on to trains.

Many modern freight trains carry whole containers. This means that freight can pass from ship to train to truck without ever leaving its container, saving the costs and time of unloading and repacking. Many piggyback services go even further. Laden trucks drive onto a train to be carried for part of their journey. After reaching the correct railroad stop, the truck simply drives off the train and on to its final destination. Piggyback systems are important in the United States, where they decrease travel time by days for long-distance journeys.

SIGNALING

A high-speed train takes more than 2 miles (3.2 km) to stop, so accurate signaling is an essential part of a safe railroad. The most widespread system is called Automatic Block Signaling, which was invented by Thomas Hall in 1967. This system divides a railroad into lengths, or blocks, about 1 mile (1.6 km) long. An electric current flows along just one rail for the length of an empty block. When a train enters the block, however, the current flows through the train's metal wheels electrifying the other rail. This change in current alerts a controller or computer, and alters the signals to stop all other train from rolling into the block. These signals are delivered with red,

Railroad controllers can see where every train is on a rail network using a graphical display. If delays or accidents occur, controllers can redirect trains to other lines. The diagram below outlines the block signaling system used to keep trains a safe distance from each other.

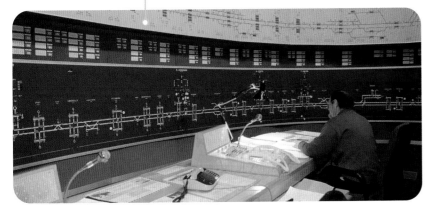

1

1) The gray train has a green signal so the driver can travel into at least the next two blocks.

2

2) As the train passes the first signal, the green light turns red. The next light is yellow, showing driver that next one will be red.

3

3) As the train passes the second light, it turns red. The first light turns yellow. Since another train is in the block ahead, the third light is red, signaling the driver to stop.

4

4) The driver passes the red by mistake, and an alarm sounds in the cab as a warning. The first light is green again since the two blocks ahead are now clear.

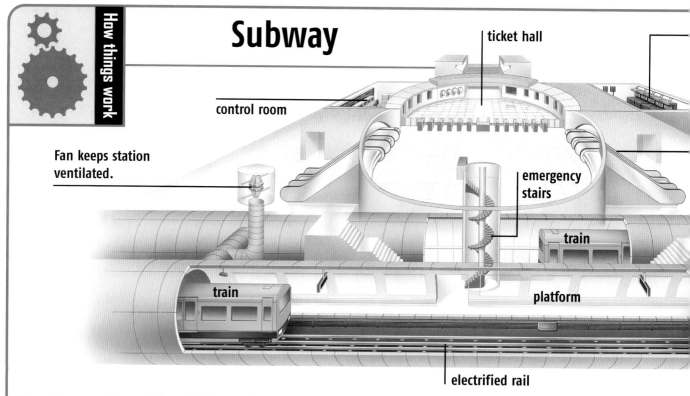

Subway

control room

ticket hall

Fan keeps station ventilated.

emergency stairs

train

train

platform

electrified rail

The subway systems of New York, London, and Tokyo are among the most complicated railroad networks on Earth, used by millions of passengers every day. The New York City network is the biggest, with some 137 miles (220 km) of underground track and another 93 miles (145 km) above ground. Subway systems operate a number of different train lines, that fan out to all corners of the city, many of them sharing sections of track in the center. For this reason, signaling systems must be sophisticated and secure. The first subway was opened in London in 1863 to ease congestion on the city streets. Subways are now built in cities where space is at a premium, and where the cost of land makes it worthwhile to tunnel underground. The original London subway was powered by steam trains, which gave way to the first electrically powered subway, known as the *Tube*, in 1890. In modern subways, power is usually supplied by an electrified third rail.

yellow, and green lights beside the track, or through on-board computers in the driver's cab.

Busier networks with several connected lines use Continuous Cab Signaling. Here, a computer in front of the driver gives the signal. A control center collects information about the speed and position of all trains. This is used to calculate a safe speed for each train, which is sent to the driver. A safe speed could be anything from a full stop to full speed. Modern trains have extra protection from Automatic Train Protection, or ATP, which brakes the train if the driver exceeds the recommended speed limit or passes a red signal.

TRACK

The basic methods of track construction have not changed since the 19th century. A firm foundation to carry the train's weight is essential. This is built on a thick layer of gravel called ballast, which is laid over the bare ground. Wooden or concrete

Track designs have changed little over the last 150 years. Early railroads, such as the Union Pacific, had tracks with wooden ties. The rails were held in place by spikes. More modern tracks have concrete ties, with the rails held on by metal clips.

Electricity supply is distributed through a substation.

Passengers reach platform by escalators.

A rail gang position the ties of a replacement section of track. They are using a machine that runs over the new track on temporary rails.

blocks called ties are set into the ballast. Lengths of steel rail are fastened to the ties with metal clips or long spikes.

The fundamental design of railroad track may not have changed, but many innovations have improved train safety and speed. Since the 1950s, engineers have welded lengths of rail together into one continuous piece of metal. This gives a smoother and quieter ride, removing the *clackety-clack* sound. The precision of the track has also been improved greatly. Where modern railroads run around corners, for example, the outside track is positioned slightly higher than the inner one. This means the train leans into the turn, making it less likely to derail (leave the track) at high speeds.

Track maintenance is a huge expense for any railroad company. Weedkiller trains are dispatched up and down the track regularly to spray the ballast and keep plants off the rails. Track recorders monitor the rails for problems, and a team of maintenance staff are always on hand to fix any lumps, breaks, or blemishes.

flange

wheel

rail

tie plate

wooden tie

spike

subsoil

ballast

axle

concrete tie

rail clip

HIGH-SPEED TRAINS

Today we take speeds of 125 mph (200 km/h) or more for granted on long distance trains. Faster travel has been a priority for train operators since the days of the first passenger services. Fast trains make for satisfied customers, and enable operators to run more journeys each day.

One of the first purpose-built high-speed train services was introduced in Britain in 1935. The steam-powered *Silver Jubilee* traveled between Newcastle and London at speeds of up to 112 mph (181 km/h)—then a world record. *Silver Jubilee* was beaten three years later by the *Mallard*, another British train, which reached a speed of 126 mph (202 km/h). After this, the speed competition went global. In 1955,

the French railroads put two of their latest electric locomotives through their paces. One engine reached a new world-record speed of 205.7 mph (331 km/h). The following day, the other locomotive matched the speed exactly.

BULLET TRAINS

By the 1960s, train companies were under greater pressure than ever to attain higher speeds on long distance routes. Railroads were now competing with passenger aircraft, which were carrying people faster than ever. In addition, advances in car design and many new highways made road transportation faster, too. The first true high-speed services of the modern age were launched in Japan in 1964, in

A bullet train whizzes through the Japanese countryside. These electric-powered trains were the first to run regular services at 130 mph (209 km/h) when introduced in 1964.

time for the Tokyo Olympic Games. The *Shinkansen*, meaning "new railroad," used the latest electric locomotives to carry passengers at 130 mph (209 km/h). The sleek *Shinkansen* rolling stock became famous around the world as the bullet train, initially operating between Tokyo and Osaka. The latest bullet trains currently reach speeds of 186 mph (300 km/h), although there are plans to raise this limit to 217 mph (350 km/h) in the near future.

While Japanese rail engineers concentrated on electric engines their French counterparts were using gas turbines to power trains. Jet engines used to power aircraft are gas turbines, but those developed for trains did not push them forward with a jet of hot gas. Instead, the stream of gas is used to generate electric power to turn the train wheels. However, despite initial successes, these engines proved to be very expensive to run, especially when oil prices are high.

A TGV speeds along track in France. These trains are the fastest locomotives in regular use.

The French created a more lasting train legacy in the form of the electric *Train à Grande Vitesse* (TGV)—literally "high-speed train" in French. This is currently the fastest passenger train in the world. During normal service it cruises at speeds of nearly 200 mph (322 km/h) and in tests it has rocketed along at 320 mph (513.3 km/h). TGVs and most other high-speed trains are driven by electric motors, housed within power cars at the front and back of the train.

WEIGHT AND SHAPE

Weight is an important factor in the design of high-speed trains. Both new materials and building techniques can cut the weight of a train by many tons, helping it travel faster. Most trains are made of steel, a strong metal that can be made into thin sheets. But aluminum plate is an even better material. A 16-car aluminum train weighs more than 222 tons (200 metric tons) less than a steel train of the same size. Aluminum does not rust either, so there is no need to add extra weight in the form of protective paint.

Fast trains are given another speed boost by their aerodynamic shape. This ensures that as much energy as possible goes into forward motion rather than pushing air out of the way. Slow trains have a boxy appearance and flat, square noses. When they move quickly, swirling eddies of air move back along the carriages creating air resistance, or drag forces. Air particles trapped between and under rail cars also increases the drag.

High-speed trains look very different. Their profile is designed to disturb the air as little as possible and reduce drag. This means a pointed nose, a smooth underside, and small spaces between the carriages. Air passes smoothly over such streamlined trains, even at high speed. As well as being more efficient, the trains are also much quieter.

Air is always going to present some problems for fast-moving trains. When a train speeds into a tunnel, for example, air is squeezed between the train and tunnel walls. If this high-pressure air forces its way into the cars, it can damage fittings and hurt passengers' ears. For this reason, air vents in high-speed trains are automatically closed when they enter tunnels. High-pressure shock waves also means the tracks on high-speed railroads have to be placed wide apart. Otherwise, the air flowing around trains traveling in opposite directions would collide. On a normal railroad, this blast of air could be strong enough to knock passing trains from the rails.

SLOWING DOWN

Brakes are essential safety features of all trains, and they need to be particularly effective for high-speed models. A train traveling at 168 mph (270 km/h) takes up to

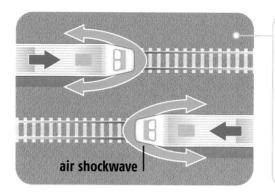

air shockwave

High-speed trains must travel on tracks that are farther apart than most. The extra space provides room for the air to move past other trains.

Acela Express

On straight track the train is upright.   **A turning train tilts into the bend.**

The Acela Express is the fastest train service in America. It travels between Washington and Boston with a top speed of 165 mph (266 km/h). Like other high-speed trains, Acela Express locomotives receive power from overhead cables. They also have a sophisticated suspension system that tilts the train as it speeds through the many sharp curves on the line. On the stretch between New York and Boston alone, the track makes the equivalent of 11 full circles.

The Acela's six passenger cars are designed to reduce the tilt force felt by passengers. This prevents travelers from being thrown against windows or into the aisle as the train makes turns. The Acela rail cars are kept level by air and coil springs installed underneath that tilt the passenger car the opposite way to the suspension. Hydraulics hold the cars at the correct angle. Each car has its own automatic control unit, and tilts independently of others.

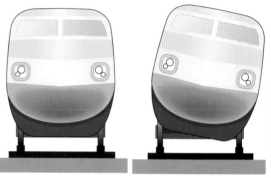

An Acela Express train.

High-Speed Trains

How things work

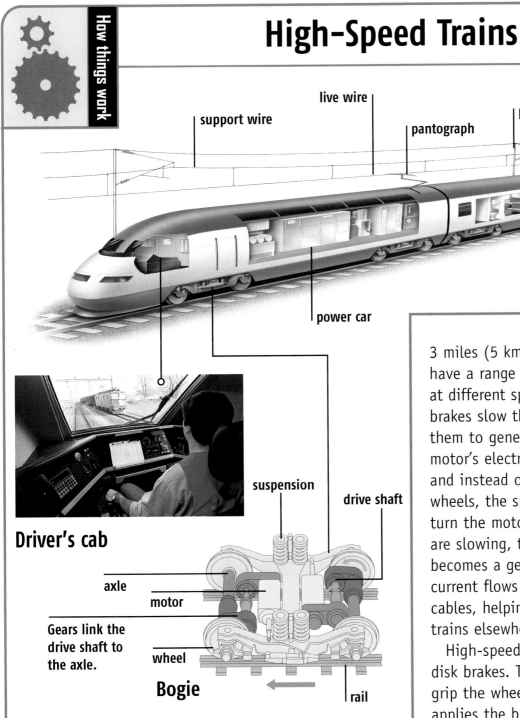

support wire

live wire

pantograph

pylon

passenger cabin

power car

Driver's cab

suspension

drive shaft

axle

motor

Gears link the drive shaft to the axle.

wheel

rail

Bogie

The French TGV, or *Train à Grande Vitesse*, is the most popular design of high speed train in the world, and cruises at speeds of nearly 200 mph (322 km/h). The TGV has been exported to many countries, including Germany and South Korea. TGVs also run through the under-sea Channel Tunnel between France and Britain. TGVs are electric trains with motors in each bogie (wheel set; above). They draw power from overhead cables, through a pantograph. The pantograph must be positioned exactly. If it pushes too hard on the cables, they wear away, but a connection that is too light will not draw enough current.

3 miles (5 km) to stop. Trains have a range of brakes for use at different speeds. Regenerative brakes slow the wheels by getting them to generate electricity. The motor's electricity supply is cut and instead of it turning the wheels, the spinning wheels turn the motor. While the wheels are slowing, the turning motor becomes a generator, and electric current flows back into overhead cables, helping to power other trains elsewhere on the line.

High-speed trains also have disk brakes. These circles of steel grip the wheel when the driver applies the brake, slowing them down by friction. A third type of brake, the tread brake, runs a band between the train wheel and track, reducing the friction between the two. This has the effect of making the wheels spin without moving the train forward very effectively. Tread brakes are only used at slow speeds.

MAGLEV

An artist's impression of a maglev train service that is being built in Shanghai, China. The Transrapid trains will have an electromagnetic maglev design.

An alternative form of rail power was invented in the 1960s. Magnetic levitation, or maglev, trains and the track they travel on are giant magnets. The train does not touch the track but floats above it, held in midair by strong magnetic forces opposing one another.

Because they do not touch the track, maglev trains travel without any friction forces slowing them down and can achieve very high speeds. Experimental maglev trains have been developed for many years, but they are still too expensive for long distance or high-speed lines. The longest public maglev line currently in use is 19 miles (31 km) long and connects Orlando, Florida, to Disney World. Like other services around the world, these trains travel at low speeds. High-speed maglev systems are being planned in Tokyo and Germany, however.

There are two types of maglev train. The first is called electrodynamic maglev. A Japanese train of this type hit 300 mph (480 km/h) on a test track—the fastest speed ever reached by a train. Electrodynamic maglev uses superconducting magnets.

(Superconductors carry electric current without wasting any energy. They only work when cooled to low temperatures.)

The magnets are installed along the bottom of the train. As the train magnets pass coils in the track, they induce electric currents in the coils. Once electrified, the coils also produce a magnetic force that pushes against the train's magnets. Once it reaches high speeds the train rises 4 inches (10 cm) above the track. The train is pushed along by a wave of magnetic force. This wave is produced by another series of coils in the track, which carries electric pulses.

Electromagnetic maglev trains work in a different way. This system was developed in Germany in the 1970s, and it is the one used for the world's few commercial maglev lines. Electromagnetic maglev trains fit around a T-shaped guideway. Instead of pushing each other apart, the magnets on the train and track pull toward each other, raising the train a fraction of an inch (1 cm) above the track.

Electromagnetic Maglev Train

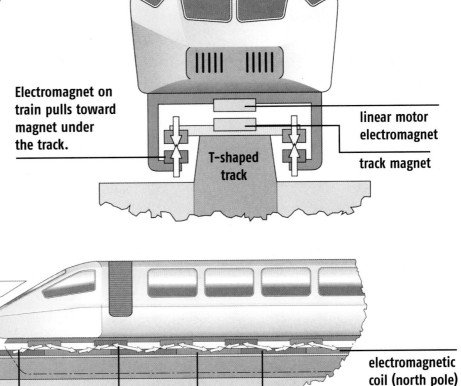

Electromagnet on train pulls toward magnet under the track.

linear motor electromagnet

track magnet

T-shaped track

PROPULSION

Maglevs are propelled by linear induction motors. These consist of a line of electromagnet coils under the train. Electromagnets are only magnetic when electrified. The electromagnets in a maglev track can be switched between north and south poles by changing the direction of the current. When the currents in alternate magnets are repeatedly switched, a wave of magnetic force flows along the train. This wave interacts with magnets along the track. Forces of attraction and repulsion move the train forward at high speed.

electromagnetic coil (north pole)

attraction force

repulsion force

track magnets

electromagnetic coil (south pole)

THE FIRST CARS

The first mechanical engines appeared in the 18th century. At the time, traders and travelers relied on the strength of their animals to transport themselves and their belongings, but many people began to imagine carts driven by engines.

ON THE ROAD

The first powered land vehicles bore no resemblance to modern cars. The only engines invented at the time were driven by steam power. These were at an early stage of development, based on original designs used to pump water out of mines.

In 1769, French engineer Nicholas Joseph Cugnot (1725–1804) succeeded in scaling down a steam engine to a size small enough to power a road vehicle. Nonetheless, the resulting "steam carriage" was cumbersome and moved at very slow speeds.

Other inventors were inspired by Cugnot's efforts and set about improving his design. By the 1800s the engine design had been improved enough to power a small network of steam-powered buses in Paris. Steam engines were also being used for road transportation in the United States, where two New Englanders, Nathan Read and Apollo Kinsley, both ran steam vehicles in the 1790s.

In England, inventor Richard Trevithick (1771–1833) built his first steam-driven carriage in 1801. The new vehicle ran at speeds of

An early Mercedes race car that won the French Grand Prix in 1908. The driver maintained an average speed of 69.5 mph (111 km/h) throughout the race. Mercedes cars were built by one of the inventors of the automobile, Gottlieb Daimler. In 1926, his company merged with that of Karl Benz, who was also one of the first car designers.

between 4 and 9 mph (6 and 15 km/h), and had driving wheels 10 feet (3 m) across. Trevithick took his steam carriage for a drive through the streets of central London. The prototype, however, was overtaken by horse-drawn carts or even by people walking at a fast pace. Frustrated by his apparent lack of success on the road and inspired by new iron railroads, Trevithick decided that

steam-powered vehicles were not ready to replace horse power on the streets and turned his considerable talent to trains.

HEAVY WORK

Other inventors were prepared to stay on the road. Beginning in 1831, Englishman Walter Hancock built a series of steam-powered machines that traveled at speeds of 20 mph (32 km/h)—a world

Cugnot's Wheeled Carriage

Key inventions

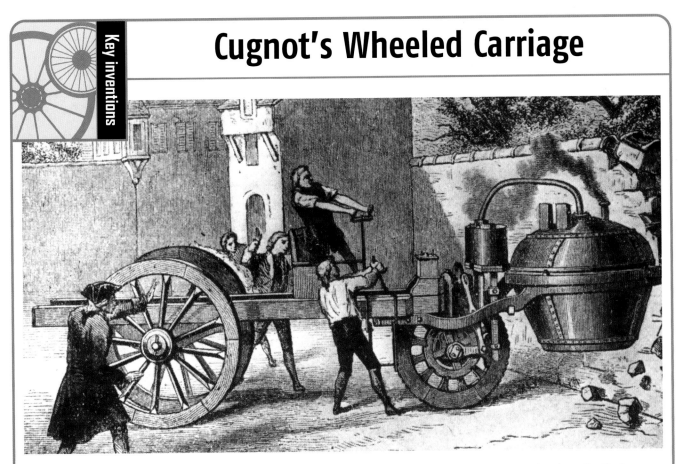

The first road vehicle to be powered by an engine was the three-wheeled carriage invented by French military engineer Nicholas Joseph Cugnot. The frame of Cugnot's vehicle was a gun carriage. It was powered by a steam engine, suspended from the carriage's wooden frame. High-pressure steam was used to drive a shaft attached to the carriage's front wheel. Any dreams of high-speed battle wagons or powerful road vehicles were

dented when the carriage crashed on its first journey in 1770. During a demonstration in Paris, the carriage reached a speed of 2 mph (4 km/h). The carriage (above) was so hard to steer that it crashed into a wall before running out of steam after only 15 minutes. Despite this setback, Cugnot had captured the imagination of his military bosses. They ordered a version to pull cannons, although the design was never used.

A steam tractor built in the 1890s connected to wagons. Steam-powered vehicles were mainly used to pull heavy loads along roads.

land-speed record at the time. Hancock built a fleet of these machines to compete with horse-drawn omnibuses as public transportation in London.

However, the very nature of steam power ruled out a long-term future in road transport. Steam engines are dirty, heavy, and inefficient, and could not travel along the roads in any great numbers. These facts were recognized even in the early 19th century, when the toll charges for steam-powered vehicles shot up on the back of pollution, noise, and opposition from horse riders. Hancock's bus service was run out of business by 1836.

Steam carriages persisted in some cities. The first practical steam-driven truck worked in Glasgow, Scotland, in the 1870s. In 1892, steam delivery vans took to the streets of Paris. Although dreams of steam-powered cars were over, the engines were still useful for transporting heavy freight. Steam trucks were used by some breweries and coal salesmen right through to the 1920s.

Steam-powered vehicles were more practical in the countryside, where they took the hard work out of plowing fields. By the late 19th century, steam-powered tractors and other farm machinery were becoming common in Britain. On the North American prairies, settlers used steam vehicles to make a profitable living out of vast tracts of fertile land. In many countries, steam also powered the traveling circuses of the time.

ALTERNATIVES TO STEAM

It was clear that vehicles small and fast enough for private travel would require another source of power. In the last twenty years of the 19th century, two engineers completed an extraordinary period of invention to lay the foundations for all modern cars. The internal-combustion engine was developed separately by German engineers, Gottlieb Daimler (1834–1900) and Karl Benz (1844–1929). Their new engines were smaller, lighter, and more powerful than the steam engine, using a series of carefully controlled fuel explosions to power pistons and turn wheels.

The combustion engine was a breakthrough, but its inventors also had to design a vehicle that made the most of the motor. One of the most important ancestors of modern cars was actually a motorcycle. After building a combustion engine, fueled by benzene—a flammable liquid found in petroleum oil—Daimler constructed a wooden bicycle frame to test it out on. Completed in 1885, the design was similar to modern motorbikes in having the engine mounted between the two wheels and driving the rear wheel. Daimler's bike was also fitted with small stabilizer wheels, which helped riders stay upright on bumpy streets at slow speeds.

As Daimler concentrated on motorcycles, his rival Karl Benz put his energy into mounting a combustion engine on a more stable tricycle. Benz's early design, which was also finished in 1885, is generally accepted as the first real car. The tricycle had its first public outing in Benz's home town of Mannheim, Germany in July, 1886, when it reached a speed of 9 mph (15 km/h).

People and society

Inventing the Car

The internal-combustion engine is the most important invention in the history of motoring, and several people had a hand in developing it. The first combustion engine was thought to be made in England in 1820, but Belgian Étienne Lenoir was the first to use an engine to power a carriage in 1862. His vehicles were fueled with lamp gas, and the Czar of Russia was one of several people who bought one. Austrian inventor Siegfried Marcus fitted an engine to a handcart (above) in 1870, and Frenchman Edouard Delamare-Deboutteville put a gasoline engine into a chassis in 1883.

However it took the German engineer Karl Benz to bring out the best of the internal-combustion engine. Before Benz, many engineers had failed to build practical vehicles. Benz was the first to build a useful, self-propelled road vehicle and started the automobile industry. A little more than a century later, tens of millions of car are driven on every continent.

The internal-combustion engine sparked a road revolution. By now people were using gasoline—a much less harmful fuel than benzene—to power the engines. Automobile production quickly spread to other countries, and in 1895 the first vehicle with a fully enclosed engine was built in France. Many of the car manufacturers founded at this time, such as Benz, Daimler, Peugeot, and Oldsmobile, are still household names today.

DESIGN DEVELOPMENTS

With the basics of engine and body design out of the way, inventors turned their attentions to making the cars travel faster. The engines of the earliest cars turned wheel axles with a large chain, similar to those used in bicycles. Transmission systems were developed to link engine power directly to drive shafts, making higher speeds possible. Brake pads that gripped the whole wheels were developed to improve safety in faster vehicles.

Following the ideas of John Dunlop, who had fitted pneumatic (air-filled) rubber tires to his son's bicycle a few years before, engineers at Peugeot, a French automobile maker, built an experimental car with similar tires in the 1890s. The air-filled tires proved to grip the ground better, and more of the engine's power was converted into forward movement. The tires also made for a less bumpy ride.

This Peugeot automobile went on to compete in a race from Paris to Bordeaux 1895. The tires had to be changed 22 times in the 750-mile (1,200-km) journey. The car's driver, Edouard Michelin, went on to found the famous Michelin tire company.

Other improvements followed to make motoring safer. By 1906, drivers could enjoy the benefits of windshields made from glass, fenders, and rear-view mirrors. By this time, gasoline-driven vehicles were being used for public transportation, but private cars were still an expensive hobby for the wealthy. It took the commercial instincts of the famous American businessman Henry Ford to bring motoring to ordinary people.

A French racing automobile fitted with Michelin tires is depicted in wall tiles taking part in a 1902 race from Paris to Vienna. The word automobile *was first used in France, taken from the Latin for "self" and "moving."*

62

The Benz Victoria

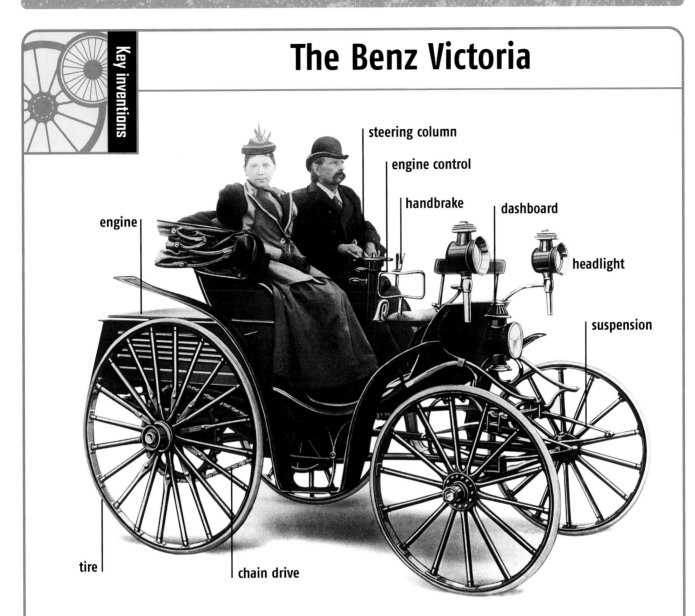

engine

steering column

engine control

handbrake

dashboard

headlight

suspension

tire

chain drive

After building an internal-combustion engine into a tricycle in 1885, Karl Benz turned his attention to four-wheeled automobiles. These were the first cars to make driving a practical possibility in both city streets and country lanes. Benz designed the basics of brakes, gears, and steering in order to produce the Benz Victoria in 1893. At the time, vehicles were designed to be pulled by horses. Coachbuilders worked on the body of the Victoria, giving it the same large wheels and high driver's seat of a cart. Consequently Benz's first cars were known as horseless carriages.

Their light wheels and slow speeds meant they could be steered with a small tiller, placed on a column in the middle of the car. Driving a Benz Victoria (above, driven by Benz with his daughter

Clara) was not easy, however. Benz installed a simple accelerator in the form of a lever that moved back and forth, jolting the car into a higher speed. There was no brake pedal, and although the car ran to a halt in a short time when the engine was cut, it was fitted with a handbrake that clamped brake pads against the wheel rims. This brake lever required considerable strength, and weaker drivers had difficulty stopping the car.

Benz's early cars bumped along on spoked bicycle wheels or on heavy wheels adapted from carts. The ride became more comfortable with the introduction of air-filled pneumatic tires, but car drivers regularly had to stop to fix punctures. Despite these problems, Benz's cars soon became the playthings of Europe's wealthiest families.

MASS PRODUCTION

The industrialist Henry Ford (1836–1947) combined his engineering skills with a strong business sense to create the first great car company. Ford built his first car, named the Quadricycle, in 1890. This vehicle had the same design as horseless carriages, resembling a cart more than a modern car. He spent a lot of time and effort building his cars, selling them at a high price.

He founded the Ford Motor Company in Detroit, Michigan, in 1903 and initially built cars that only the rich could afford. These high production standards were normal among most car manufacturers in America and Europe, but they did not make for high profits. In the early 20th century, less than 62,000 vehicles were produced worldwide every year, with almost half of them built in France.

Ford changed conventional patterns of car production and ownership forever in 1908, when he struck on the idea of a mass-produced car. He used an assembly line to produce a single model of car, the now-famous Model T, in huge numbers. Ford saved money by manufacturing many of the cars' components himself. Each car produced was more or less identical so they could be produced quickly and cheaply.

> *One of Ford's time-saving techniques was to have components brought to the correct point on the assembly line from other parts of the factory by conveyor. Here cylindrical fuel tanks, arriving overhead, are being fitted to the chassis.*

Henry Ford stands between the first car he ever built, the Quadricycle (right) and the ten millionth Model T to leave his factory (left).

Before the assembly line was introduced in 1913 a Ford took six hours to construct. By 1925, the line made one car every 10 minutes.

Ford famously quipped that his customers could have a new car in "any color they like, as long as it's black."

By 1913, each Model T began life at one end of a 352-yard (320-m) assembly line. Teams of workers along the assembly line repeated the same pre-set tasks, such as fitting engines, welding doors, or painting bodywork, for every car. After every stage of assembly, the cars moved forward on a conveyor to the next work area, where another stage was begun. Between 1908 and 1927, 15 million Model T cars drove out of the Ford factory, at a rate of 14,000 a week.

Ford passed on the money saved by his manufacturing techniques to his customers. In 1908 a Model T cost $950, much less than any of its competitors but still more than most families could afford. With further savings one million Americans owned a Ford by 1913, and by 1920, half the cars in the world were Model Ts. By 1926, the Model T cost just $290, putting it within the reach of the average American family.

HOW CARS WORK

Car ownership in the developed world is at an all time high. In the United States alone there are more than 150 million cars, one for every 1.8 people. Modern cars are reliable, fast, and comfortable, and manufacturers are constantly seeking innovations to make their models stand out from the rest. Engineers have greatly improved engine efficiency, lowered fuel consumption, and created air-conditioned interiors. Modern cars are equipped with entertainment systems, automatic gear changes, and even navigation aids that tell drivers where they are.

POLLUTION PROBLEMS

Government regulations have also played an important role in shaping modern car design.

Although modern cars use far less fuel per mile than earlier designs, the sheer number of cars today creates pollution problems, which affect people's health and contribute toward climate change. Governments tackle these issues with laws controlling what a car can burn as fuel and what it can emit in its exhaust. Car manufacturers have responded to these challenges by developing cleaner fuels and engines.

A lot of effort has been devoted to developing pollution-free cars that could be powered by the energy in sunlight or hydrogen gas, but so far, nothing has been developed that can rival the gasoline-powered internal-combustion engine for fast and inexpensive road transportation.

Every automobile, from this high-speed coupe to a minivan, works in the same way. All have internal-combustion engines powered by gasoline or diesel, and all need brakes, a steering system, and transmission to work properly.

INTERNAL COMBUSTION

From large family cars to subcompacts, most automobiles are powered by gasoline-burning engines. These convert the energy released by burning a mixture of gasoline and air into mechanical movement that is used to turn the wheels. In other words, cars are driven by a rapid series of controlled fuel explosions.

At the heart of most car engines are four metal cylinders. The up-and-down movements of the piston inside each cylinder ultimately turns the wheels of the car. As each piston moves down its cylinder, it sucks in the gasoline and air mixture through an intake valve. When the piston reaches the bottom of its cylinder, the valve closes and the piston starts to move back up.

The next down stroke of the piston is driven by the ignition of gas and air. As the piston nears the top of the cylinder, the volatile fuel mix is squeezed into a smaller space. At this point, the mixture is ignited by an electrical device called a spark plug. The mixture explodes, driving the piston back down into the cylinder. As the piston rises again, it expels any waste gases through an exhaust valve as it does so.

The cycle then begins again with the piston drawing in fresh fuel and air for the next explosion. (*Continued on page 70.*)

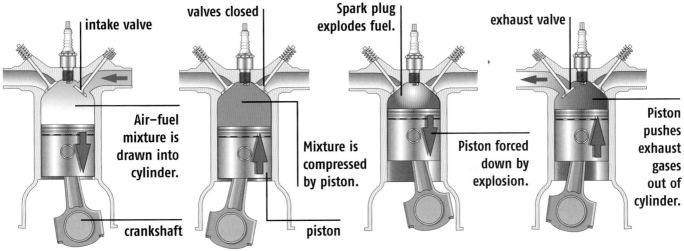

Stroke 1: Piston drops | Stroke 2: Piston rises | Stroke 3: Piston drops | Stroke 4: Piston rises

The four-stroke cycle of a gasoline engine. Cars have at least four cylinders, and each one cycles independently. At all times every stage of the cycle is occurring inside an engine.

The up and down motion of the pistons is converted to rotational motion by the crankshaft.

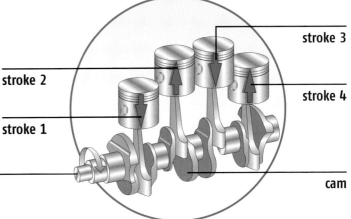

INSIDE A CAR

Each car is made up of around 14,000 different parts. The body is usually made from molded steel. The car's body is joined to the frame, or chassis, and supports the engine, transmission, fuel tank, suspension, steering, and brakes.

In the United States alone, seven million people work in the automotive industry. Many of them help to design and build new cars. However, many more work as mechanics, maintaining and fixing the country's millions of cars.

radio antenna

seat belt

The exhaust gases are released in a steady stream by the muffler.

The exhaust gas flows out from the tailpipe.

Brake lights warn following drivers that the car is slowing.

Suspension

The hub cap covers the nuts that connect the wheel to the car.

fuel tank

The catalytic converter removes harmful pollution from the engine exhaust.

shock absorber

brake drum

suspension spring

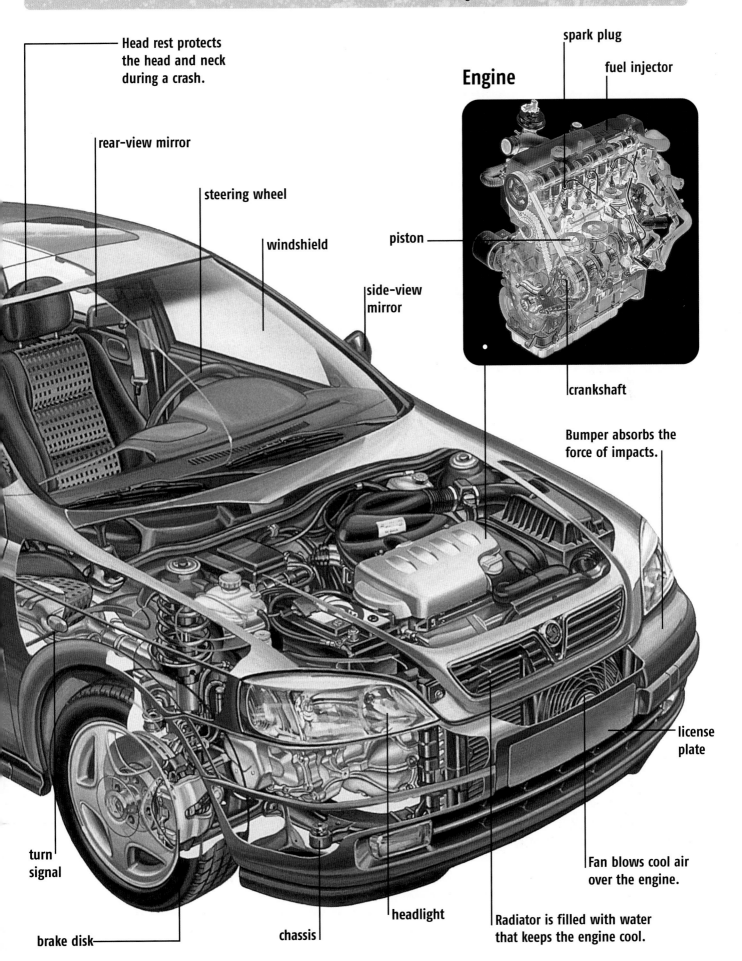

Head rest protects the head and neck during a crash.

rear-view mirror

steering wheel

windshield

side-view mirror

spark plug

fuel injector

Engine

piston

crankshaft

Bumper absorbs the force of impacts.

license plate

turn signal

Fan blows cool air over the engine.

brake disk

chassis

headlight

Radiator is filled with water that keeps the engine cool.

Engine action can be summarized in four points—fuel intake, fuel compression, ignition, and exhaust—resulting in a four-stroke cycle. The pistons are kept lubricated by a supply of oil, and kept cool by a series of fans and water reserves.

Diesel engines, which are fueled by diesel oil, a heavier fuel than gasoline, have a similar four-stroke cycle to gasoline engines. Instead of drawing in fuel and air, however, the pistons in diesel cylinders just draw in air, which is then squashed until it becomes very hot. At this point, diesel oil is sprayed into the cylinder. The oil burns rapidly in the hot air and drives the piston down. Diesel engines are more efficient than gasoline ones, although they cannot be used to reach very high speeds. They are generally fitted to large vehicles like trucks, while gasoline engines drive cars.

TRANSMISSION

The up-and-down movement of the pistons is turned into rotary movement by a part of the engine called the crankshaft. Each piston is connected to this rod by a cam, an egg-shaped wheel. The crankshaft runs horizontally through the center of the engine and also controls the opening and closing of valves. The pistons rise and fall at different times so one piston is always being driven down by an explosion. The force of this piston keeps the other pistons in the engine moving through the other three strokes.

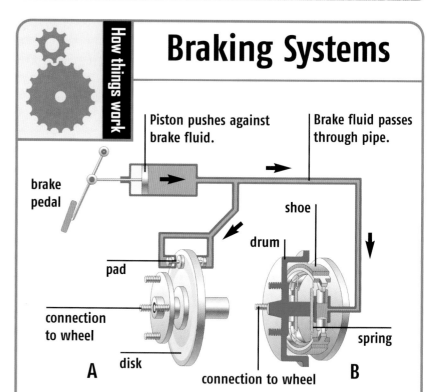

How things work

Braking Systems

Piston pushes against brake fluid.

Brake fluid passes through pipe.

brake pedal

shoe

drum

pad

connection to wheel

disk

A

connection to wheel

spring

B

Today's cars are fitted with powerful brakes. Drivers of the first cars were not so lucky. Then, the only brakes were pads that pressed on the rim of the wheel and were operated by a brake lever. Whether or not the car stopped in the distance required depended on the strength of the driver. Fortunately, the first cars did not move very fast, but better brakes became essential as car engines improved.

The brake pedal in modern cars is linked to the brakes by pipes filled with oil. This system takes advantage of hydraulics—the scientific laws that govern fluids. These laws state that the pressure of a liquid in a closed container is equal throughout. In other words, liquids cannot be squashed into a smaller space. So when a force is applied to a liquid at one end

of a pipe, the liquid instantly applies the same force at the other end. When a brake pedal is pressed, it pushes an oily brake fluid through tubes and into the brake. The oil filling the brake causes it to grab the wheel and stop it from turning.

Most modern cars are fitted with disk brakes (A) at the front and drum brakes (B) at the rear. Disk brakes have pads that pinch a disk joined to the wheel to slow it down. Drum brakes contain shoes that press outward to stop a hollow "drum" attached to the wheel from spinning. Springs pull the shoes away from the side of the drum when the brake is released.

Cars may also be fitted with a computer-controlled antilock braking system (ABS). These prevent skidding by releasing the brake on any locked wheel.

Tire treads vary according to where they will be driving. Deep treads provide grip in mud, while smooth tires work best on wet roads.

The rotary motion of the crankshaft is carried through a gearbox to the tires by the drive shaft. The gearbox, a system of intermeshed wheels, or gears, controls how fast the wheels are turned by the engine. Together,

the gearbox and drive shaft are described as the transmission because they "transmit" the engine's motion to the wheels.

In many cars, the transmission drives a single pair of wheels, either the front or back. The unpowered wheels turn on their own as they are pushed or pulled along by the driven wheels. In four-wheel-drive vehicles, such as jeeps, all wheels are connected to the engine to give better grip and control on rough terrain.

IN AND OUT

The four-stroke engine is all about precision. The wrong mixture of gasoline and air sucked into the engine at the wrong time means anything from less efficient fuel use to a dangerous explosion. To combat these risks, modern engines use a computer-controlled pump to inject just the right amount of fuel into the engine. This is known as fuel injection and replaces a less precisely measured system used in older cars called a carburetor, which mixed the gasoline and air before it reached the cylinders.

The gases produced when fuel burns are released through the exhaust system. The burning of gasoline and air in engine cylinders has damaging side-effects, producing carbon dioxide and water along with sulfur dioxide, nitrogen oxides, and other compounds, many of which cause asthma and other respiratory diseases.

Key inventions

Catalytic Converter

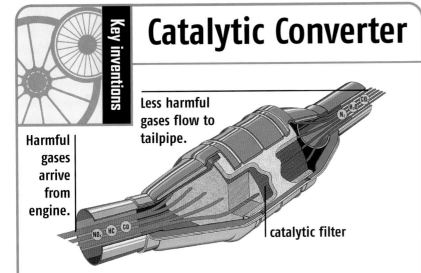

Less harmful gases flow to tailpipe.

Harmful gases arrive from engine.

catalytic filter

Catalytic converters are used to break down pollution in car exhausts into less harmful waste products. The catalytic converter is fitted inside a widened part of the exhaust pipe. Exhaust gases are forced through fine filters containing platinum and rhodium. These metals cause the exhaust gases to react with each other, re-forming into harmless gases. These are released from the exhaust pipe into the air. New cars are fitted with a converter by law, but converters are not perfect. Pollution still gets through to the atmosphere.

Besides threatening the environment, the burned fuel–air mix presents dangers for the car itself if not removed properly. The exhaust gases must be pushed out of the engine's cylinders before a new supply of gasoline and air is drawn in. If not, the fresh mixture will not ignite properly and the engine will eventually stall. So the exhaust pipe is a vital part of the car engine, and it must be kept clean. The engine's exhaust valve is affected by a muffler, which lets the gases out steadily rather than in several noisy spurts. The gases are then released into the open air at the rear of the car through the tailpipe.

BODYWORK

A car's engine, brakes, wheels, and exhaust are fitted on to a strong metal frame called a chassis. The body is assembled by welding sheets of steel to the chassis to form the roof, hood, and doors. The shape of car bodywork has changed substantially over the years. The first mass-produced automobiles were shaped like boxes. As cars picked up speed, designers realized that boxlike shapes slowed vehicles down since they dragged through the air. Engineers developed new, aerodynamic designs that do not disturb air so much at higher speeds, making for a more fuel-efficient and stable journey. Over the last century, cars have moved closer to the ground and become much more streamlined.

Robust suspension is another vital part of controlling modern cars. Car tires are air-filled to make for a smoother ride. The tread of the tire—the area that contacts the road—is especially thick, with grooves cut into the rubber that help grip the road and clear water out of the way.

Thick, strong springs between each wheel hub and the car body keep all four tires on the road when the car travels over uneven

Modern car plants are filled with hi-tech equipment. As in Henry Ford's revolutionary Detroit plant, cars are built on assembly lines (above), but much of the work is done at high-speed by robots (left).

Power Steering

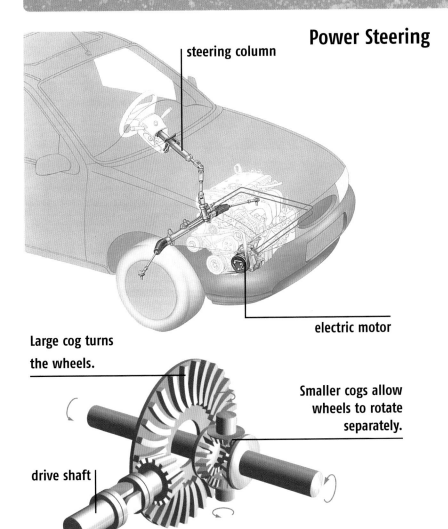

steering column

electric motor

Large cog turns the wheels.

Smaller cogs allow wheels to rotate separately.

drive shaft

Differential Gear

surfaces or turns corners. Shock absorbers prevent the springs from bouncing too much and keep the car body as steady as possible. Without suspension, cars would be almost impossible to control at high speed.

Most cars have power steering. When the driver turns the steering wheel, he or she does not have to physically turn the front wheels. Instead, an electric motor moves them, making it easier for the driver to steer a heavy vehicle.

As the car turns a corner, the inside wheels need to travel a shorter distance than the outer

ones. The differential gear is an assembly of cogs that allows one wheel to spin at a slightly different speed than the other. Thanks to the differential gear, outer wheels can spin faster and not skid when a car speeds through a sharp corner.

INTERIOR DESIGN

Innovation has also progressed inside of the car. The leather-upholstered, climate-controlled interior of a modern luxury car is a far cry from the flimsy rain roofs and high, awkward seats of the first horseless carriages designed by Karl Benz. On the car floor, carpet absorbs engine and road noise and keeps feet warm. Specially designed seats offer support for the back and neck. Passenger and driver seats can be moved backward and forward to give drivers enough legroom to operate pedals and make passengers comfortable.

Drivers have a range of information displayed to them from dials and screens positioned behind the steering wheel and on the dash. The speedometer tells them the speed, for example, and other gauges show engine activity and fuel levels. The word *dash*—the driver's console—harks back to the first days of driving. The dash or dashboard was named more than 100 years ago for the boards on horse-drawn carriages that stopped coachmen being dashed by stones tossed up by the horses' hooves.

How Transmissions Work

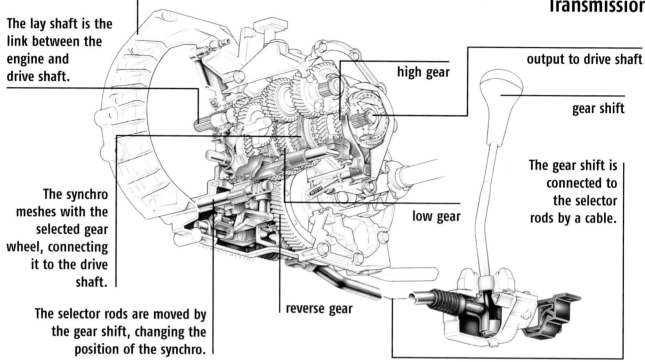

The clutch housed inside this casing grips a flywheel turned by the crankshaft. When the clutch pedal is pressed, the clutch lets go of the flywheel, breaking the connection between the engine and gears.

Manual Transmission

The lay shaft is the link between the engine and drive shaft.

high gear

output to drive shaft

gear shift

The synchro meshes with the selected gear wheel, connecting it to the drive shaft.

low gear

The gear shift is connected to the selector rods by a cable.

The selector rods are moved by the gear shift, changing the position of the synchro.

reverse gear

Most cars have four or five forward gears and a single reverse gear. The lower gears are used for pulling away from a stop and climbing steep hills, while higher gears are used for increasing speed and cruising on open roads. The gears are part of a car's transmission system—the parts that take power from pistons moving up and down in the engine and use it to turn the wheels.

A gear is a wheel with teeth that meshes with a second wheel. If both gear wheels have the same number of teeth, they turn at the same speed with equal power. If one wheel has twice as many teeth as the one that drives it, the larger wheel turns at half the speed but with twice as much power. Likewise the speed is doubled and power halved if a wheel drives another gear with half the number of teeth.

Inside a car, the rotary motion of the engine's crankshaft is used to spin one of several gear wheels inside the transmission. This gear is linked to the drive shaft, which turns the car's wheels.

The larger the gear wheel, or cog, selected, the less distance the car wheels travel for every turn of the crankshaft. Cars are started up with a large cog— first gear—to direct all the engine's power into getting the stationary vehicle to begin moving. Once the wheels are turning, the second gear is engaged, followed by higher ones as the car speeds up. Each higher gear wheel is smaller than the previous one. With each upward gear change, the car's wheels turn around more times with every cycle of the engine.

Most cars in North America have automatic gear shifts, which select gears according to speed and gradient without the driver having to do anything. European cars, however, have manual gears operated by the driver. The driver uses a clutch pedal to disengage the drive shaft from the last gear and selects another gear using the gear shift. Releasing the clutch reconnects the engine. In both automatic and manual gear systems, the driver always selects the reverse gear manually.

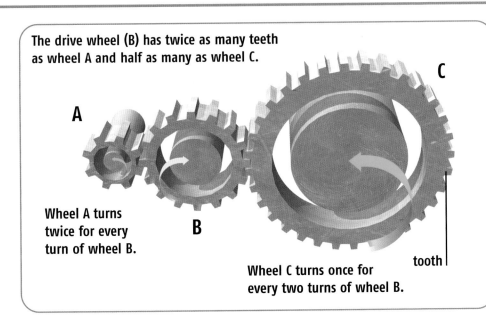

The drive wheel (B) has twice as many teeth as wheel A and half as many as wheel C.

A

B

C

Wheel A turns twice for every turn of wheel B.

Wheel C turns once for every two turns of wheel B.

tooth

Automatic Transmission

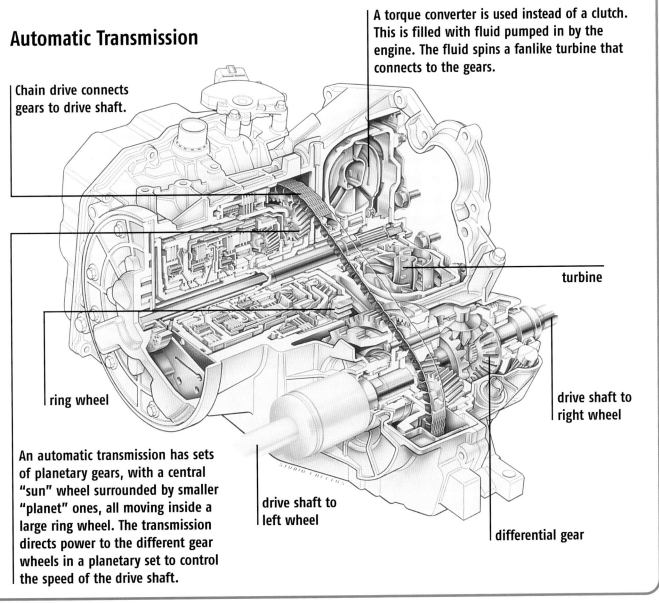

A torque converter is used instead of a clutch. This is filled with fluid pumped in by the engine. The fluid spins a fanlike turbine that connects to the gears.

Chain drive connects gears to drive shaft.

turbine

ring wheel

drive shaft to right wheel

An automatic transmission has sets of planetary gears, with a central "sun" wheel surrounded by smaller "planet" ones, all moving inside a large ring wheel. The transmission directs power to the different gear wheels in a planetary set to control the speed of the drive shaft.

drive shaft to left wheel

differential gear

75

SAFETY

The design of any new model of car owes as much to safety as it does to speed. Seat belts are one of the most common safety devices, and have been a required car part for many years. Seat belts are fitted to an inertia reel, which allows the wearer to move around freely during a normal ride. Any jerk on the seatbelt, such as in a crash, causes it to lock. This prevents people from flying forward as the car stops suddenly.

Airbags are another safety feature. These are also activated by sudden impacts, and pop out of the dash or steering wheel, inflating in a fraction of a second. Airbags prevent head injuries by absorbing the force of the driver being thrown forward.

CRUMPLE ZONES

Cars are designed to prevent injury and death by absorbing the force of a crash before it reaches the driver and passengers. Some cars fulfil this with specially reinforced bodywork that absorbs crash impact. Others have bodies designed to crumple on impact. Crumple zones in

The moment of impact during a crash test. The dummy in the front seat detects the forces a human driver would experience if his or her car crashed in this way. Crash-test dummies are designed to behave just like a human body.

A dummy is flung into an inflating air bag. The bag is blown up with gas that is produced when pellets are ignited in the event of a sudden impact.

the hood and trunk of the car absorb the energy of the crash before it travels to the driver. Although these cars appear totaled after a crash, such a flexible design actually improves the occupants chances of survival.

DUMMY PASSENGERS

Safety features must pass vigorous tests before reaching the production line. Car manufacturers run a series of crash tests, which simulate real-life dangers such as head-on collisions. With crash-test dummies in the seats, cars are slammed into walls as computer-linked instruments monitor how every force, stress, and strain travels through the car body and its dummy occupants.

Computer simulations have taken over from many of the crash tests, so that engineers have a good idea about what will happen to a new design of car before they run a physical impact test.

Ultimately, much of a driver's safety is in his or her own hands. Speed limits, road signs, and traffic signals are all designed to keep cars a safe distance away from each other. The majority of crashes are still caused by careless driving and not by a fault with the car. Safe braking distances between cars traveling on highways are often ignored, sometimes with fatal results. People driving too close to each other cannot stop in time to avoid accidents ahead and cause multiple pile ups.

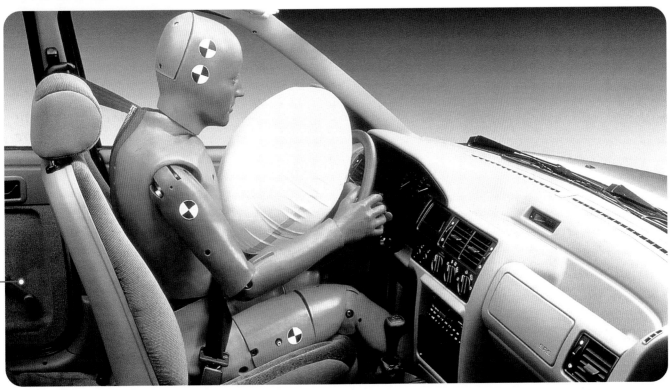

MOTORCYCLES

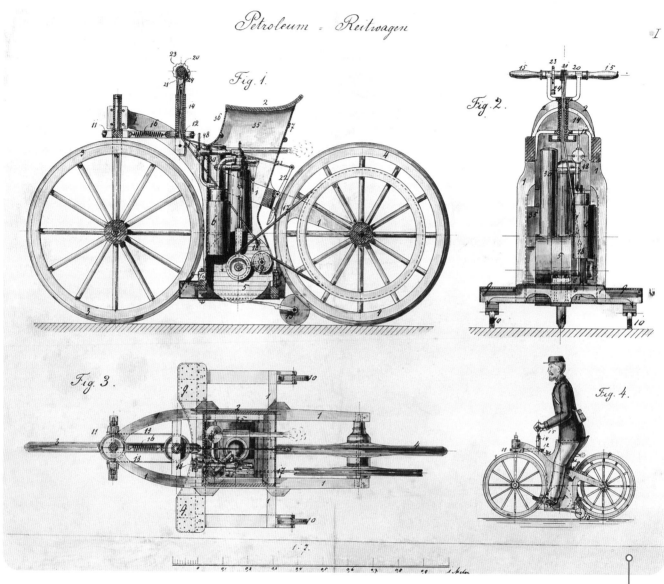

Petroleum = Reitwagen

Fig. 1.

Fig. 2.

Fig. 3.

Fig. 4.

Mopeds and motorbikes are popular alternatives to automobiles in many countries, and a good way of beating traffic congestion. The size of a motorcycle engine is indicated in cubic centimeters (cc; 0.06 cubic inches). Mopeds have an engine capacity of 50 or 100 cc, while the most powerful motorcycles have engines of 1,000 cc or more—as large as the engine of a small car.

Modern motorcycles are started by electronic ignition. Older models are kick-started with a lever by the rider's footrest. The engine works in the same way as a car. However, the crankshaft is connected to the back wheel

A design of the world's first motorcycle, built by Gottlieb Daimler in 1885. The motorcycle was actually invented before the automobile.

by a chain drive via a gearbox. The front wheel is not driven by the engine, but turns at the speed set by the rear.

Motorcycle designers make the best use of available space, and the whole engine takes up much less room than car engines. The fuel tank is located directly behind the handlebars. There are often storage spaces under the seat.

Riders operate the bike's controls with hand and foot levers. A twist-grip on the right handlebar acts as a throttle, accelerating the bike. The gear shift is located on the left handlebar or by the driver's foot. The disk brakes on each wheel are operated by levers on the handlebars.

Motorcycles are more dangerous than cars. In accidents, riders have little protection. Many bikers take the precaution of wearing protective leather clothing and helmets. The bikers' leathers will help them slide over the ground if they fall and limit their injuries.

Bikers wear a helmet to protect their head in accidents. Their leather suits and strong boots are also used to keep the riders safe if they fall.

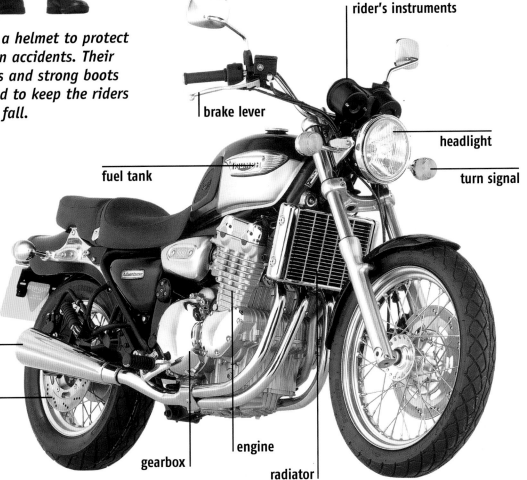

rearview mirror

rider's instruments

brake lever

headlight

fuel tank

turn signal

tailpipe

brake disc

engine

gearbox

radiator

ON TRACK AND OFF ROAD

A great variety of vehicles are built around the basic design of the automobile, all of them adapted for different jobs, from racing to digging in quarries.

THE BIG PRIZE

Cars have been used for sport since the early days of motoring. These first races were between owners of the same models of car driving through city streets. Today, motorsport inspires the most sophisticated car design in the world. The pinnacle of car races are the Formula One (F-1) *Grands Prix* (Great Prizes). These races take place on specially built circuits around the world from Monaco to Australia. Spectators pack stadiums to see the world's greatest drivers race at speeds in excess of 190 mph (305 km/h).

As a family car, an F-1 racer would be useless. It has one seat, no radio, and a huge appetite for fuel. Rather than comfort, racing cars are built purely for speed. That means the best possible aerodynamics and road-hugging design. The body of a racing car is shaped like a tube, a design called a monocoque. The car sits close to the ground, helping it cut through the air easily.

Formula One cars travel so fast that they would take off like an airplane it it were not for the upside-down wings mounted on the front and rear of the vehicle

Automobiles come in all shapes and sizes. The largest and smallest are used just for fun. A single wheel of this mighty monster truck dwarfs the motorized trike.

Indy Car

Indy cars are raced in oval speedways in the United States. Their design is similar to Formula 1 cars. Indy cars drive faster than 200 mph (320 km/h) and are named for the Indianapolis 500, a 500-mile (805-km) race.

1. The car's wings create forces that push the car on to the ground.

2. The engine is positioned behind the driver. It is fueled with methanol.

3. The car's cockpit is designed to protect the driver during a crash.

4. The soft rubber tires help the car cling to the road. However, they wear out quickly and need to be replaced during long races.

Racing cars are not the fastest vehicles on Earth. The land-speed record is held by the Thrust SSC (SuperSonic Car). In 1997, this car broke the sound barrier reaching 763 mph (1,227 km/h) in the Nevada desert. Equipped with two fighter-jet engines, the Thrust SSC has the power of 145 Formula One cars.

that push the car back onto the road. The car's curved body also guides air around the sides, preventing it from traveling underneath the car. Since air does not get underneath, a partial vacuum is created, which helps hold the high-speed car on the road. In terms of aerodynamic movement, the cars' large wheels may look like a disadvantage. In fact, they stabilize the vehicle and are essential for gripping the road when drivers negotiate tight corners at high speed.

OFF ROAD

Rally car racing is another popular motorsport. Rally cars are a type of off-road vehicle that are adapted to cope with steep hills, mud, and water that would be too much for less powerful cars. Off-road vehicles are fitted with four-wheel drive. Engine power travels to all four wheels rather than just the back or front two, helping the car to get over uneven surfaces.

Improved grip is the other key to the off-roader's success, ensuring that all four wheels stay on the ground to make the most of the well-distributed engine power. Extra wide tires with very deep treads make short work of

Tanks can cross just about any terrain except the steepest mountains. Unlike rubber tires, tracks cannot be punctured.

climbing hills and muddy stretches because more of each tire is in contact with the ground at any time. Rally cars also have more lower gears than a standard car, and this helps drivers put extra engine power into overcoming obstacles. Despite these features, crashes are an everyday hazard for off-road racers. Rally cars are fitted with a roll cage—a tough steel structure that protects the driver if the car turns over.

MAKING TRACKS

For some vehicles, improved wheel grip is not enough. Military tanks and heavy construction machines have ridged caterpillar tracks running over a series of modified wheels, providing unrivaled grip. Unlike normal wheels, they are in contact with the ground for the whole length of the vehicle.

The controls used to steer a tracked vehicle are very different from these of a normal steering wheel. Two levers in the cab control the power and direction of each track. To turn the machine, the driver reduces the power to one track so it turns more slowly than the other. This makes the whole vehicle reel around.

Tanks are an impressive piece of hardware. Their reinforced metal bodywork protects soldiers from fire, bombs, and water. But perhaps the most famous military vehicle is the jeep, the original utility vehicle. The first jeeps were designed in response to a request for a new general purpose vehicle issued by the U.S. army in 1940. The Ford Motor Company was one manufacturer that responded to the challenge, with GP, or *General Purpose*, vehicles. "GP" soon became "jeep."

With their robust frame and sturdy wheels, jeeps went on to become the workhorse of the U.S. military. With some engineering imagination, jeeps were adapted to become equipment carriers and ambulances. One version could travel on water, and another prototype was even fitted with rotor blades so it could fly into battle towed behind an airplane!

DIGGING AND DUMPING

Mobile construction machines have revolutionized the way we build roads, bridges, and houses. Most of the tools used today, such as pulleys and levers, date back thousands of years. While our ancestors used animals or people to power these systems, engineers of today have more mechanical muscle available.

Many smaller construction machines operate on wheels rather than tracks, or use a mixture of both. The tires are typically very wide and tall. This spreads the weight of the machine more evenly over the ground and prevents slippage or sinking into soft earth. Some vehicles are fitted with retractable steel struts called outriggers that are thrust into the ground for extra stability when lifting heavy loads.

The power transmission in heavy construction machines is also reinforced. Engines and other moving parts are often linked together by a strong chains, rather than gear wheels. This ensures there is no slippage and power loss when the machine is laboring under heavy loads.

One of the most versatile construction machines is the backhoe loader, which can perform several construction chores, such as digging and clearing soil. Both ends of the machine mean business. The front arms are equipped with a shovel-like loader, which can be used to push rubble aside, or lift up dirt and rock. The attachment at the rear is called a backhoe, a small arm-and-bucket excavator that uses a bucket with sharp steel teeth to dig out soil.

The backhoe and loader have several joints and are moved into position with hydraulic pistons. The driver uses a series of levers to control each part of the machine. A single engine is used to power the wheels and digging machinery.

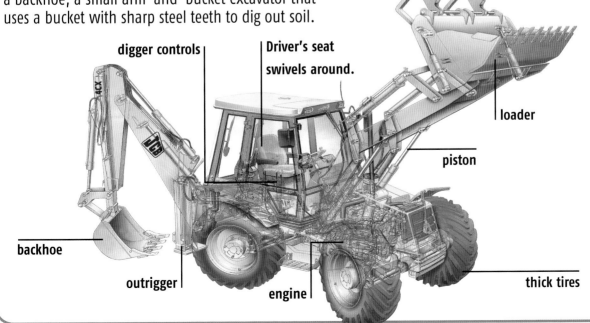

digger controls

Driver's seat swivels around.

loader

piston

backhoe

outrigger

engine

thick tires

ROCKET MOVER

fuel tank

Atlantis

rocket booster

launch platform

crawler-transporter

control room

track

The Kennedy Space Center in Florida is home to some of the most remarkable machines on Earth. This is where new engine types are pioneered aboard space rockets that would never leave the ground on conventional fuel mixtures. Instead, space shuttles lift off on explosive combinations of hydrogen and oxygen.

However, NASA's spacecraft need a goliath rocket mover to reach the launch pad.

Crawler-transporters carry spacecraft from huge assembly buildings to the launch sites on Cape Canaveral. Powered by enormous diesel engines, a crawler-transporter does not match space shuttles for fuel innovation, but is remarkable simply for its size. Each transporter is 131 feet (39 m) long and 114 feet (34 m) wide. The transporter platform is some 20 feet (6.1 m) above ground level.

The Space Shuttle **Atlantis,** *attached to its huge fuel tank and rocket boosters, inches its way toward the launch pad aboard a giant crawler-transporter. NASA has two transporters, which began work in the 1960s. Since then the transporters have traveled more than 2,500 miles (40,000 km), equivalent to a trip from the space center to Los Angeles, California.*

launch tower

The machine's two huge engines generate enough electrical power to operate the on-board motors that are used to steer the transporter.

Space vehicles are placed upon their launch platforms before they set off to the pad. A crawler-transporter is driven underneath this platform and picks it up. The transporter moves on four double-tracked crawlers spaced 90 feet (27 m) apart at each corner. The tracks (above) are 10 feet (3 m) high and 41 feet (12 m) long. A single link on the track weighs 1 ton (906 kg).

The crawler is well-named. It takes five hours to make the trip to the launch pad at a top speed of about 1 mph (1.6 km/h). The transporters travel on a roadway that is 130 feet (39 m) wide. This road goes up a slight incline leading to the launch pad. The crawler-transporters are fitted with hydraulic arms that keep the platform flat all the time. This levelling system keeps the tall rocket or space shuttle from toppling over. The crawler also needs large supplies of fuel. A fully laden transporter burns 150 gallons (568 liters) of diesel every mile. A car uses one thirtieth of a gallon to cover the same distance.

The crawler transporter was originally developed for the Apollo Moon missions. In those days the mighty vehicle carried huge Saturn V rockets.

CARS OF THE FUTURE

People are always on the move and so are their imaginations. From the horse-drawn carriages that dominated 19th century streets to today's choice of cars, trains, and planes, engineers have been constantly developing faster and more specialized forms of transporting people and products.

The last century has seen an explosion in the number of private cars. This car revolution was powered by gasoline, but supplies of oil will eventually run out or create too much environmental damage. When cars burn fuel they release pollution that causes lung diseases or contributes to climate changes. So what will power the transportation of the future?

CLEANER FUELS
Current candidates for alternative fuels range from cleaner burning petroleum alternatives like natural gas—cooled into a liquid so it can be pumped into fuel tanks more easily—to more exotic plans for solar power or electricity that rethink the whole internal-combustion engine.

Other cleaner fuels include biodiesel and ethanol. Biodiesel is made from vegetable oils and animal fats. Unlike fossil fuels, it comes from renewable energy sources and reduces emissions of carbon monoxide, sulfates, and unburned, sooty hydrocarbons associated with gasoline. It is simple to convert a gasoline engine to run on pure biodiesel, and the new fuel is available at the pumps in several countries.

Ethanol is the scientific name for the intoxicating chemical in alcoholic drinks. It is produced by fermenting starchy crops, such as sugar beet and sugar cane. When mixed with gasoline, ethanol improves the quality of engine emissions, and more than 1.5 billion gallons are added to gasoline in the United States every year. In some places, this fuel mixture can even be

A streamlined solar-powered car races through the Australian desert. The energy in sunlight is converted into electricity by panels on the car's roof. The electricity powers the wheels.

The pumps used for fueling cars powered by liquified petroleum gas (LPG) are very different to regular gasoline pumps because the fuel is stored in the tank under high pressure.

purchased as gasohol. Ethanol can make up between 10 and 85 percent of the fuel supply depending on the type of car.

NO POLLUTION

Hydrogen gas is also being explored for use in combustion engines. It is a simple and light fuel that yields no pollution. Hydrogen is produced by splitting water into its constituents—hydrogen and oxygen—using electricity. When hydrogen burns it combines with oxygen in the air to make water again, so nothing has been wasted or emitted.

There are still many obstacles to overcome before hydrogen becomes a readily available fuel that is safe and easy to use. It takes a lot of energy to extract it from water, and hydrogen cannot simply be poured into a gasoline tank. It exists normally as a gas and is difficult to store or transport. Storage systems being

developed include compressed hydrogen, liquid hydrogen, and bonding the gas to a solid material. Many scientists believe the most promising future for hydrogen in transportation is via in-car electricity generators called "fuel cells." These cells combine hydrogen fuel with oxygen from the air to produce an electric current which powers the car.

ELECTRIC CARS

Opening the hood of an electric vehicle, whatever its power supply, reveals a very different sight to the pistons and valves of a regular car—there is no engine and no exhaust. Electricity is unique among alternative fuels in that it is a direct source of mechanical power. Whereas fuels like gasoline and ethanol only give up their chemical energy when they are burned in a combustion engine, an electric motor turns car wheels directly.

From the outside, a hybrid car might look the same as one fueled by gasoline. But inside the car has not just a regular internal combustion engine, but also an electric motor, a large battery, and even a generator that can convert the car's motion into electricity for storage. All these make hybrid cars very efficient.

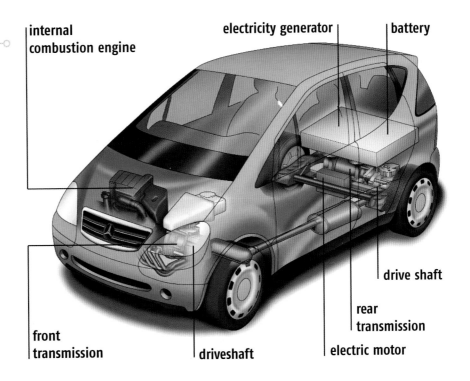

internal combustion engine — electricity generator — battery — drive shaft — rear transmission — electric motor — driveshaft — front transmission

Fuel cells are one possible way of powering electric vehicles. However, electric vehicles on today's production lines run on energy stored in batteries, and this electricity will have to be generated in a regular power plant, burning polluting fuels to do so—although more efficiently than a car. There are thousands of battery-powered vehicles on U.S. roads already, many of them converted from gasoline. Depending on battery material and car design, electric vehicles can run between 50 and 130 miles (80 to 209 km) before needing to be plugged into the main electricity supply for a recharge.

Electric vehicles are particularly suitable for modern city lifestyles, where the need for pollution-busting transportation is greatest. With their low speeds and zero emissions, electric vehicles are perfect for making short trips along congested city streets. Research shows that half of all car journeys last less than ten minutes, and electric vehicles are more suitable for these activities than gasoline-powered cars.

HYBRID ENGINES

The most promising alternative to gasoline engines are hybrid cars that use both battery-powered engines and a normal gasoline engine. Although they still use gasoline, they are more efficient and can travel more than 50 miles to the gallon (20 km/liter).

Hybrids are so efficient because when they are accelerating the electric motor works alongside the gasoline engine. When the car is slowing down, the gas engine shuts down, and the rotary motion of the slowing car wheels is used to generate electricity and recharge the car's battery. Hybrid cars are already on sale and will no doubt be an important new technology for the future of road transportation.

SUNSHINE TRAVEL

Electric vehicles have great potential, but the most promising option for clean road and rail transportation is perhaps solar power. Our local star is the biggest powerhouse in the solar system. Even from a distance of 92 million miles (148 million km), the Earth is bathed in phenomenal amounts of heat and light energy from the Sun.

The problem is how to harness these forms of energy and turn them to mechanical power.

Cars have had a huge effect on society because they allow people to go wherever they want, whenever they want. However, when everyone wants to travel at the same time, such as during the rush hour (below), traffic jams can make journeys last a long time.

Global Positioning System

Poor map readers need never be lost again with the spread of in-car navigation devices, which tell confused drivers exactly where they are—and how to get to their destination.

These dashboard devices connect to the Global Positioning System (GPS), which is now used by thousands of civilian drivers. GPS was originally developed for the U.S. military at a cost of $12 billion. Much of this money was spent on the building and launch of a network of 24 satellites that constantly orbit the Earth. Signals from these satellites can be used to pinpoint the location of any GPS receiver on the planet to within a few feet.

GPS uses an ingenious system called triangulation to calculate position. At any one time, five to eight satellites are visible to receivers from any point on the planet. The rest are concealed from radio contact by the curvature of the Earth. The distance to each of the

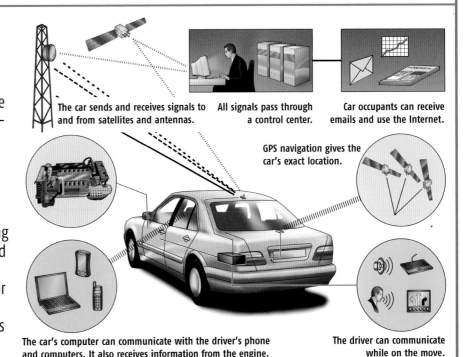

The car sends and receives signals to and from satellites and antennas.

All signals pass through a control center.

Car occupants can receive emails and use the Internet.

GPS navigation gives the car's exact location.

The car's computer can communicate with the driver's phone and computers. It also receives information from the engine.

The driver can communicate while on the move.

visible satellites is measured according to the time it takes for radio signals from satellites to reach the ground. The exact position of the satellites is always known, so if the signal time corresponds to 12,000 miles (19,312 km) for one satellite and 11,000 miles (17,703 km) for another, the GPS receiver must be closer to the second satellite. By cross-referencing data from several satellites in this way, the location of the receiver is narrowed down to give its

precise coordinates. Because radio signals travel at 186,000 miles (299,338 km) a second, users can get their location almost instantaneously.

Many modern cars are fitted with GPS technology. As well as providing a location-finder, navigation systems can also access information about traffic conditions and plan short cuts around traffic jams. Drivers are guided to their destination by a computer screen or by following voice instructions.

Solar panels are notoriously inefficient. They rely on clear weather and are more suited to powering the occasional light bulb than firing up a whole car.

This does not prevent engineers from trying. There are now several well-established motor races for cars running directly on solar

power. This includes the 1,864 mile (3,000 km) World Solar Challenge coast-to-coast trip in Australia, and the 2,300 mile (3,701 km) American Solar Challenge between Chicago and Los Angeles—a long way to travel in cars reaching an average speed of 40 mph (64 km/h).

Time Line

6000 B.C.E.
The harnessing of animals to haul loads helps Middle Eastern people to construct the first cities.

2000 B.C.E.
The first bridges are built.

1115 B.C.E.
Assyrian Empire begins first organized road building.

1550
First wooden rails built in mines.

1804
Richard Trevithick demonstrates one of the earliest steam trains on new iron tracks, reaching a speed of 5 mph (8 km/h).

6,000 B.C.E.   1700   1800

1286 B.C.E.
Hyksos people use horse-drawn war chariots.

1500
Hungarian wagon builders design coach.

100 C.E.
First wooden framed horse saddle developed by Sarmatian people of Asia.

1789
William Jessop invents points system for railroads.

1769
James Watt patents powerful new type of steam engine to make steam driven trains feasible.

1817
German inventor
Karl von Drais invents
the first bicycle.

1880s
German engineers
Gottlieb Daimler and
Karl Benz develop the
internal-combustion
engine and produce
the first automobiles.

2003
Hybrid cars
go on sale.

1830
First U.S. passenger
railroad service opens.

1902
The first mainline electric
train service opens in Italy.

1908
The U.S. Ford Motor Company
launches the world's first
mass-produced car.

1900

2000

1869
U.S. completes
its first
transcontinental
railroad.

1930s
Diesel-electric
locomotives
are introduced.

1863
First subway system
opens, in London, England.

1997
The Thrust SSC car
sets a new land
speed record of 763
mph (1,227 km/h),
in Nevada.

1839
Kirkpatrick MacMillan
invents the pedal bike.

Glossary

Alternative fuels The term used to describe alternatives to polluting fossil fuels.

Automatic Block Signalling A system designed to reduce the risk of trains colliding.

cable car A type of streetcar pulled along by a moving cable running between the rails.

calliper brakes A braking system commonly used in racing bicycles, whereby blocks squeeze the wheel rim to slow it down.

catalytic converter Part of the car exhaust system which removes some of the harmful chemical compounds created in the burning of fossil fuels in the engine.

coach Horse-drawn coachs owe their name to the Hungarian village of Kocs, where wagon builders improved the stability and comfort of passenger carriages in the 15th century.

collar harness Design of harness that puts the weight of the load on the animal's shoulders.

diesel-electric locomotives The power car in this design uses diesel fuel to generate electricity, which in turn powers the train.

disk brake Type of brake used in trains, cars and bikes. Disks pinch the wheel to slow it down.

drum brake Brakes that contain two brake shoes that press outwards to stop a hollow metal "drum" in the wheel.

gauge The term used to describe the width of railroad tracks.

gears A transmission system for taking the turning power of engines or pedals to the wheels.

internal-combustion engine An engine that uses a series of carefully controlled fuel explosions to power a series of pistons.

maglev Magnetic levitation rail locomotive.

piggyback services Trains that carry entire road trucks as freight.

points system Short, tapered lengths of rail used to guide trains between different tracks.

stage coach Long-distance passenger service in which journeys were broken up into short stages.

skidoo Motorized snowmobile.

skis Plates used to slide over snow.

yoke A simple design of harness, consisting of two pieces of wood shaped as a cross.

Further Resources

Books

The Art of the Automobile: The 100 Greatest Cars by Dennis Adler. HarperResource, 2000.

The Best Book of Trains by Richard Balkwill. Larousse Kingfisher Chambers, 1999.

Web Sites

Smithsonian: Aviation and Transportation
http://www.si.edu/science_and_technology/aviation_and_transportation/

DaimlerChrysler
http://www.daimlerchrysler.com/

Railroad History Database
http://rrhistorical.com/rrdata/

Index

Page numbers in **bold** refer to feature spreads; those in *italics* refer to picture captions.

Picture Credits